This is Your Mother

This is Your Mother

The scriptural roots
of the Rosary

Ronald Walls

GRACEWING

First published in 2003

Gracewing
2 Southern Avenue, Leominster
Herefordshire HR6 0QF

ISBN 0 85244 403 6

Typeset by Action Publishing Technology Ltd,
Gloucester GL1 5SR

Printed by
Antony Rowe Ltd,
Eastbourne BN23 6QT

CONTENTS

Part Four: The Glorious Mysteries

Preface

On the cross our Lord Jesus commended the beloved disciple, John to his mother, Mary. John received this privilege not for himself alone but as representative of all 'the rest of her children' (Revelation 12.17) that is, all whom the Father has adopted in Jesus Christ.

When praying the Rosary we invite the blessed Mother of God to show her care for us. At the wedding feast in Cana, to which her Son accompanied her, Mary's initiative prepared the way for him to 'let his glory be seen'. As we seek her company by praying the Rosary, she helps us contemplate the mysteries of our Faith and look upon the glory of her Son.

Mary was steeped in the written and oral traditions of her people, and so more than any other is able to guide us towards a fruitful reading of the Scriptures; such reading deepens our grasp of the Faith, which is what we try to do as we meditate upon the mysteries of the Rosary, the substance of which is the history of salvation, recorded in the Holy Scriptures. The mysteries of the Rosary are an abstract from this whole, comprising a series of episodes in the life of our Lord and of his mother.

Since the sixteenth century there have been fifteen such mysteries, divided into three chaplets – the Joyful, the Sorrowful and the Glorious. On 6 October 2002 the Holy Father, Pope John Paul II, added a fourth chaplet, which he named, 'The Mysteries of Light'. This book presents all of the twenty mysteries.

The word 'Rosary' immediately evokes the image of a set of beads; but the beads exist for the sake of the prayers which are said upon them; and the prayers are designed to guide us towards the contemplation of the substance of the mysteries. These mysteries, when studied carefully and in relation to one another, are found to contain an exposition of the story of man's salvation.

Over the past forty years or so the Rosary has suffered a decline in popularity. One of the causes of this decline has undoubtedly been the careless way in which the prayer of the Rosary has often been practised. Too often the Rosary has become a kind of prayer-wheel – an external religious action, the performance of which was felt to guarantee the acquisition of a quota of grace. Reaction away from the Rosary can, therefore, be a sign of a justifiable reaction against mechanical prayer and the tendency to think that God will hear us because of our much speaking.

But the Rosary need not be, indeed must not be, that sort of prayer. As meditation upon episodes of the gospel, it is designed to nourish the deeper penetration of the mystery of the Faith, is designed, that is, as a most true and effective means of acquiring grace through contemplation.

In his apostolic letter on The Most Holy Rosary, Pope John Paul describes Mary as the 'model of contemplation'. Pope John Paul writes: 'When at last she gave birth to him in Bethlehem, her eyes were able to gaze tenderly on the face of her Son.' The Pope continues: 'Thereafter Mary's gaze, ever filled with adoration and wonder, never left him.' When praying the Rosary we are all the time in Mary's company, sharing in her contemplation of her Son and of the mysteries he has revealed to us. Pope John Paul's letter goes on to say: 'The Rosary, precisely because it starts with Mary's own experience, is *an exquisitely contemplative prayer*. Without this contemplative dimension, it would lose its meaning'. The Pope then quotes from an Apostolic Exhortation of Pope Paul VI, delivered on 2 February 1974: 'Without contemplation, the Rosary is a body without a soul, and its recitation runs the risk of becoming a mechanical repetition of formulas'.

The Rosary is therefore admirably suited to private meditation, but even when prayed vocally in public, meditation must not be extinguished; and it need not be. St Teresa of Avila has some clear, common-sense comments to make on this very point.

> We may, of course, consider it enough to say our prayers as a mere habit, repeating the words and thinking that this will suffice. Whether it suffices or not I will not now discuss. Learned men must decide. But what I should like, daughters, is for us not to be satisfied with that alone: when I say the Creed, it seems to me right, and indeed obligatory, that I should understand and know what it is that I believe; and when I repeat the 'Our Father', my love should make me want to understand who this Father of ours is and who the Master is that taught us this prayer.
>
> You will say at once that this is meditation, and that you are not capable of it, and do not even wish to practise it, but are content with vocal prayer. You are right to say that what we have described is mental prayer; but I assure you that I cannot distinguish it from vocal prayer faithfully recited with a realization of who it is that we are addressing.
>
> (*The Way of Perfection*, chapter 24)

If this is true of vocal prayer in general, it is true of the Rosary in particular, for in the Rosary we are supposed to stretch our minds beyond the words of our prayer to the episodes in the life of our Lord and of his mother that we commemorate. Again we may turn to St Teresa of Avila for helpful comment on meditative prayer.

> By meditation I mean prolonged reasoning with the understanding, in this way. We begin by thinking of the

favour which God bestowed upon us by giving us His only Son; and we do not stop there but proceed to consider the mysteries of His whole glorious life. Or we begin with the prayer in the garden and go on rehearsing the events that follow until we come to the crucifixion. Or we take one episode of the passion – Christ's arrest, let us say – and go over this mystery in our mind, meditating in detail upon the points in it which we need to think over and try to realize, such as the treason of Judas, the flight of the apostles, and so on. This is an admirable and a most meritorious kind of prayer.

(*The Interior Castle*, Mansions 6, chapter 7)

Although St Teresa does not explicitly mention the Rosary, this quotation gives us a hint not only of the method, but of the subject matter of Rosary meditation. Note St Teresa's significant phrasing: 'We begin by thinking ... and we do not stop there ... Or we begin with ... and go on ... until ...' The subject of our meditation is the whole continuous story of man's salvation.

So often in the past, even when time has been taken to meditate upon the mysteries, people have failed to achieve their desired result because they have isolated the episodes and destroyed the continuity of the story. In this way the mysteries have become static tableaux, whereas they are incidents in a living drama. The separate scenes in isolation are like a set of still frames such as we see displayed outside a cinema. These may provide a hint of the story; but we are not satisfied until we have stepped inside and watched the whole story unfolding before our eyes. And the story told by the mysteries of the Rosary is not just a random selection of incidents in the history of man's salvation, but an exposition of the whole of that history; moreover, the story is presented within the framework of prayer, so that we are not merely trying to acquire knowledge but are seeking to become transfigured through contemplation of him from whom our salvation flows.

The script which underlies the great drama of salvation is found in the Bible, which introduces us to the characters in the drama, lets us hear what they say, and records their actions. Fruitful meditation upon the mysteries of the Rosary – 'prolonged reasoning with the understanding' of which St Teresa speaks – relies upon knowledge of the Bible; and because this is so, the prayer of the Rosary is in tune with the Church's belief that the Bible is our great source-book both of theology and of devotion.

This book provides a reflection upon each of the twenty mysteries of the Rosary, supported by a selection of Bible readings that supply some of the background which gives substance to the mysteries of the Rosary. The New Testament incident associated directly with the mystery is interpreted through the mind of the Bible, Old Testament as well as New. The Old Testament may seem to enjoy prominence. But this is not unreasonable because the alphabet of the Christian language was formed in the two millennia that preceded our Lord's coming to earth. The meditation is not a complete exposition of the biblical texts provided, but merely sufficient to stimulate meditation.

As we trace the story of mankind's salvation back to its beginnings in the time of Abraham, and as we relive in imagination episodes in that story as it unfolded down the centuries, we become much better able to appreciate the glory of its completion as presented in the mysteries of the Rosary. We learn to contemplate the face of our Redeemer with some of the understanding enjoyed by his blessed mother, Mary.

PART ONE

The Joyful Mysteries

1

The Annunciation

'I go childless': Genesis 15.1–6

It happened some time later that the word of Yahweh was spoken to Abram in a vision. 'Have no fear, Abram, I am your shield; your reward will be very great'.

'My Lord Yahweh,' Abram replied 'what do you intend to give me? I go childless.' Then Abram said, 'See, you have given me no descendants; some man of my household will be my heir'. And then this word of Yahweh was spoken to him, 'He shall not be your heir; your heir shall be of your own flesh and blood'. Then taking him outside he said, 'Look up to heaven and count the stars if you can. Such will be your descendants' he told him. Abram put his faith in Yahweh, who counted this as making him justified.

The Annunciation to Sarah: Genesis 18.1–15

Yahweh appeared to him at the Oak of Mamre while he was sitting by the entrance of his tent during the hottest part of the day. He looked up, and there he saw three men standing near him. As soon as he saw them he ran from the entrance of the tent to meet them, and bowed to the ground. 'My lord,' he said 'I beg you, if I find favour with you, kindly do not pass your servant by. A little water shall be brought; you shall wash your feet and lie down under the tree. Let me fetch a little bread and you shall refresh yourselves before going further. That is why you have come in your servant's direction.' They replied, 'Do as you say'.

Abraham hastened to the tent to find Sarah. 'Hurry,' he said 'knead three bushels of flour and make loaves.' Then running to the cattle Abraham took a fine and tender calf and gave it to the servant, who hurried to prepare it. Then taking cream, milk and the calf he had prepared, he laid all before them, and they ate while he remained standing near them under the tree.

'Where is your wife Sarah?' they asked him. 'She is in the tent' he replied. Then his guest said, 'I shall visit you again next year without fail, and your wife will then have a son'. Sarah was listening at the entrance of the tent behind him. Now Abraham and Sarah were old, well on in years, and Sarah had ceased to have her monthly periods. So Sarah laughed to herself, thinking. 'Now that I am past the age of child-bearing, and my husband is an old man, is pleasure to come my way again!' But Yahweh asked Abraham, ' Why did Sarah laugh and say, "Am I really going to have a child now that I am old?" Is anything too wonderful for Yahweh? At the same time next year I shall visit you again and Sarah will have a son.' 'I did not laugh' Sarah said, lying because she was afraid. But he replied, 'Oh yes, you did laugh'.

The birth of Isaac: Genesis 21.1–3, 6–7
Yahweh dealt kindly with Sarah as he had said, and did what he had promised her. So Sarah conceived and bore a son to Abraham in his old age, at the time God had promised.

Then Sarah said, 'God has given me cause to laugh; all those who hear of it will laugh with me'. She added:

> 'Who would have told Abraham
> that Sarah would nurse children!
> Yet I have borne him a child in his old age.'

The promise of salvation: Genesis 3.14–15
Yahweh God said to the serpent, 'Because you have done this,

> Be accursed beyond all cattle,
> all wild beasts.
> You shall crawl on your belly and eat dust
> every day of your life.
> I will make you enemies of each other:
> you and the woman,
> your offspring and her offspring.
> It will crush your head
> and you will strike its heel.'

A Jewish heroine: Judith 13.2, 6–12; 15.9b–10
They went to their beds wearied with all their drinking, and Judith was left alone in the tent with Holofernes who had collapsed wine-sodden on his bed.

She went up to the bedpost by Holofernes' head and took down his scimitar; coming closer to the bed she caught him by the hair and said, 'Make me strong today, Lord God of Israel!' Twice she struck at the nape of his neck with all her strength and cut off his head. She then rolled his body off the bed and tore the canopy down from the bedposts. Soon after, she went out and gave the head of Holofernes to her attendant who put it in her food bag. The two then left the camp together, as they always did when they went to pray. Once they were out of the camp, they skirted the ravine, climbed the slope to Bethulia and made for the gates.

Joakim the high priest and the Council of Elders of Israel came ... to see Judith and congratulate her:

> 'You are the glory of Jerusalem!
> You are the great pride of Israel!
> You are the highest honour of our race!

'By doing all this with your own hand
you have deserved well of Israel,
and God has approved what you have done.
'May you be blessed by the Lord Almighty
in all the days to come!'

MEDITATION

The first page of the Bible declares the mystery of mysteries: God, infinite and self-sufficient, has broken the silence of his own eternity and spoken, thus creating a vast and splendid universe, including man, made in his own image. Then comes the story of man's sin. Man, through pride, exchanged original righteousness for original sin; the world ceased to be a paradise and became a vale of tears.

But a glimmer of hope remained: from among the human race one would come who would bruise the serpent's head, that is, break the power of the Devil. And so the vale of tears became a place of testing, of spiritual growth, and of hope. From the twelfth chapter of Genesis onwards the Bible tells the story of the re-creation of man, the first stage in which was the calling of a particular people to be his agent in the work of redemption.

When the angel Gabriel came and spoke to Mary, the story of man's re-creation was about to enter its last chapter. And so to understand this late incident we must cast our minds back across the history of the chosen people, of whom our Lady was the final, perfect flowering. In order to make sense of what was happening to her, she must have tried to see the event in the context of the whole sequence of events through which God had been dealing with her people down the centuries. Only thus could she understand her mysterious encounter with the angel, and assess its authenticity.

In fitting herself, as a humble servant of the Lord, into the context of the history of his servant people of Israel, Mary would certainly recall Abraham, the great progenitor of her race. The angel himself guided her mind by telling her about her cousin Elizabeth, who found herself in exactly the same situation as Abraham's wife, Sarah. Abraham had obeyed God's call to leave a settled way of life in the prosperous, civilized society of Lower Mesopotamia, and accept the life of a nomad. In addition he had believed God's promise that he would become the father of a mighty nation, although, humanly speaking, that was impossible. Thus Abraham set the pattern of true religion for all time. He became father of the faithful, the friend of God; and St Paul, writing eighteen centuries later to the Christians of Rome, still harks back to Abraham: 'Abraham is our father in the eyes of God, in whom he put his faith, and who brings the dead to life and calls into being what does not exist.'

One of the chief proofs, in our Lady's eyes, that the angel's message came from God and not from Satan, was that it followed the same pattern as the message received by Abraham. There was a call to put herself completely at God's disposal, followed by a promise that seemed impossible of fulfilment in the natural course of events. She, although a virgin, was to conceive and bear a son who, as Israel's Messiah, would bring a great blessing to all the nations of the earth. As Abraham had done almost two millennia earlier, Mary obeyed the divine call and believed the promise.

Even so, the Gospel tells us, she was afraid. Strangely enough, it was the angel's apparently cheerful greeting that startled her. 'Rejoice, so highly favoured! The Lord is with you' the angel said – a phrase that is echoed in the later greeting by Elizabeth who addressed her cousin thus: 'Of all women you are the most blessed'. Something about these very words seems to have frightened our Lady.

Our Lady was startled because again she was recalling parts of the story of her people. This time we find the clue in the story of Judith – a Hollywood script if ever there was one. No wonder our Lady was startled when she received this hint of the type of role she was being asked to fill. The main part of this story (not history, but a tract for troubled times) is contained in Judith, chapters 10–13.

The tiny Jewish nation, faithful witness to the one true and holy God, was besieged by the mighty army of Holofernes, whose ambition was to bring the whole world into idolatrous subjection to Nebuchadnezzar. When the situation seemed utterly hopeless, the widow Judith, renowned for her prayer and ritual purity, set her bold plan in motion. By a ruse she gained entrance to Holofernes' camp, while assuring herself of free passage out again. On the fourth night of her stay in the camp Holofernes gave a banquet and ordered his personal servant: 'Go and persuade that Hebrew woman you are looking after to come and join us and eat and drink in our company. We shall be disgraced if we let a woman like this go without knowing her better. If we do not seduce her, everyone will laugh at us!' Judith accepted the invitation, but sat on her own rug and ate and drank provisions she had brought with her, to avoid ritual impurity. Holofernes became so excited that he drank far more than he had ever drunk before. Finally the servant got everyone out of the room, leaving Holofernes alone with Judith. By this time, however, Holofernes had collapsed in a stupor. With a prayer for strength, Judith took down the scimitar from the bedpost and hacked off Holofernes' head. She hurried off, as she had done on the three previous nights, as if to pray outside the camp. Soon the Israelites were rejoicing as the head of their mighty adversary was displayed to them, and Judith was acclaimed in these words:

> 'May you be blessed, my daughter, by God Most
> High, beyond all women on earth.

> You are the glory of Jerusalem!
> You are the pride of Israel!
> You are the highest honour of our race!

> By doing all this with your own hand
> you have deserved well of Israel,
> and God has approved what you have done.

May you be blessed by the Lord Almighty
in all the days to come!'

Now this story is an allegory; its significance lies in its spiritual meaning; Mary is Judith, the perfect Jewess, who lives by prayer and is completely pure, the ritual purity of the Old Testament being the symbol of the spiritual and moral purity of our Lady. And she is the one who 'with her own hand', that is by her free choice, has 'deserved well of Israel,' and earned the title of 'blessed in all the days to come'; she is the long-awaited seed of the first Eve, and has crushed the serpent's head, symbolized by the spectacular action of Judith in hacking off the head of Holofernes.

And so the ancient promise of Genesis was fulfilled: our Lady is the second Eve who, completely immaculate of soul, listened to the voice of God, not to the voice of the serpent, and obeyed, thus reversing the state of affairs initiated by the first Eve. Mary brought forth the Saviour of the world; she is the mother of God and mother too of the new people of God, of all Christ's brothers and sisters. Her posterity, like that of Abraham, is as the sands of the seashore in number, and all generations call her blessed.

THE ANNUNCIATION TO MARY OF NAZARETH: LUKE 1.26–38

*The angel Gabriel was sent by God to a town
in Galilee called Nazareth, to a virgin
betrothed to a man named Joseph, of the House
of David; and the virgin's name was Mary. He
went in and said to her, 'Rejoice, so highly
favoured! The Lord is with you.' She was
deeply disturbed by these words and asked
herself what this greeting could mean, but the
angel said to her, 'Mary, do not be afraid; you
have won God's favour. Listen! You are to
conceive and bear a son, and you must name
him Jesus. He will be great and will be called
Son of the Most High. The Lord God will give
him the throne of his ancestor David; he will
rule over the House of Jacob for ever and his
reign will have no end.' Mary said to the
angel, 'But how can this come about, since I
am a virgin?' 'The Holy Spirit will come upon
you' the angel answered 'and the power of the
Most High will cover you with its shadow. And
so the child will be holy and will be called
Son of God. Know this too: your kinswoman*

Elizabeth has, in her old age, herself conceived a son, and she whom people called barren is now in her sixth month, for nothing is impossible to God.' 'I am the handmaid of the Lord,' said Mary 'let what you have said be done to me.' And the angel left her.

2

The Visitation

The ark and the Ten Words: Exodus 25.10–16
'You are to make me an ark of acacia wood, two and a half cubits long, one and a half cubits wide, one and a half cubits high. You are to plate it, inside and out, with pure gold, and decorate it all round with a gold moulding. You will cast four gold rings for the ark and fix them to its four supports: two rings on one side and two rings on the other. You will also make shafts of acacia wood plated with gold and pass the shafts through the rings on the sides of the ark, to carry the ark by these. The shafts must remain in the rings of the ark and not be withdrawn. Inside the ark you will place the Testimony that I shall give you.'

The return of the ark of the covenant: 2 Samuel 6.2–3, 9–15
Setting off with the whole force then with him, David went to Baalah of Judah, to bring up from there the ark of God which bears the name of Yahweh Sabaoth who is seated on the cherubs. They placed the ark of God on a new cart, and brought it from Abinadab's house which is on the hill.

David went in fear of Yahweh that day. 'However can the ark of Yahweh come to me?' he said. So David decided not to take the ark into the Citadel of David and took it to the house of Obed-edom of Gath. The ark of Yahweh remained in the house of Obed-edom of Gath for three months, and Yahweh blessed Obed-edom and his whole family.

Word was brought to King David that Yahweh had blessed the family of Obed-edom and all that belonged to him on account of the ark of God. David accordingly went and brought the ark of God up from Obed-edom's house to the Citadel of David with great rejoicing. When the bearers of the ark of Yahweh had gone six paces, he sacrificed an ox and a fat sheep. And David danced whirling round before Yahweh with all his might, wearing a linen loincloth round him. Thus David and all the House of Israel brought up the ark of Yahweh with acclaim and the sound of the horn.

The ark is brought to the Temple: 1 Kings 8.2–10
All the men of Israel assembled round King Solomon in the month of Ethanim, at the time of the feast, and the priests took up the ark and the Tent of Meeting with all the sacred vessels that were in it. In the presence of the ark, King Solomon and all Israel sacrificed sheep and oxen, countless, innumerable. The priests brought the ark of the covenant of Yahweh to its place, in the Debir of the Temple, that is, in the Holy of Holies, under the cherubs' wings. For there where the ark was placed the cherubs spread out their wings and sheltered the ark and its shafts. These were long enough for their ends to be seen from the Holy Place in front of the Debir, but not from outside. There was nothing in the ark except the two stone tablets Moses had placed in it at Horeb, the tablets of the covenant which Yahweh had made with the Israelites when they came out of the land of Egypt; they are still there today. Now when the priests came out of the sanctuary, the cloud filled the Temple of Yahweh.

Psalms of joy in Zion: Zephaniah 3.14–18
　Shout for joy, daughter of Zion,
　Israel, shout aloud!
　Rejoice, exult with all your heart,
　daughter of Jerusalem!
　Yahweh has repealed your sentence;
　he has driven your enemies away.
　Yahweh, the king of Israel, is in your midst;
　you have no more evil to fear.

　When that day comes, word will come to Jerusalem:
　Zion, have no fear,
　do not let your hands fall limp.
　Yahweh your God is in your midst,
　a victorious warrior.
　He will exult with joy over you,
　he will renew you by his love;
　he will dance with shouts of joy for you
　as on a day of festival.

The Wisdom of God: Ecclesiasticus 24.1–11
　Wisdom speaks her own praises,
　　In the midst of her people she glories in herself.
　She opens her mouth in the assembly of the Most High,
　　she glories in herself in the presence of the Mighty
　　One;
　'I came forth from the mouth of the Most High,
　　and I covered the earth like mist.
　I had my tent in the heights,
　　and my throne in a pillar of cloud.
　Alone I encircled the vault of the sky,
　　and I walked on the bottom of the deeps.
　Over the waves of the sea and over the whole earth,
　　and over every people and nation I have held sway.
　Among all these I searched for rest,
　　and looked to see in whose territory I might pitch
　　camp.
　Then the creator of all things instructed me,

and he who created me fixed a place for my tent.
He said, "Pitch your tent in Jacob,
    make Israel your inheritance".
From eternity, in the beginning, he created me,
    and for eternity I shall remain.
I ministered before him in the holy tabernacle,
    and thus I was established on Zion.
In the beloved city he has given me rest,
    and in Jerusalem I wield my authority.'

MEDITATION

The long training of the descendants of Abraham had at last produced in Mary one who, like Eve before the Fall, was quite unspoiled by the universal sin of mankind. As in the Garden of Eden so now at Nazareth, as the angel addressed Mary, human destiny hung in the balance. Would the second Eve use her perfect freedom of will, as the first Eve had done, to resist the word of God, or would she, by love and obedience, open up the way for the Redeemer of mankind to come and save the human race? With our Lady's, 'Let what you have said be done to me,' a critical point in the story of salvation has been reached.

A fresh start had been made in the name of all mankind. Mary herself knew that this was only the start of the final phase in the story of salvation. Battle had been joined with Satan, but final victory was not yet won; the Serpent's head had been bruised, the Devil was dazed and dumbfounded, but not yet totally vanquished. The first Eve had paved the way for Adam's fall: the second Eve, by her co-operation with God, had paved the way for the advent of the second Adam, the Lord from heaven; and it is towards this mysterious and magnificent figure that our minds have already been turned in the story of the Annunciation. The Child whom Mary is to bear is announced as the mighty king of Israel, the Son of the Most High; and he is to be named Jesus, which means 'Saviour'.

To clarify her mind even more about who exactly her child

was to be, at the hint from the angel, Mary set off to consult her cousin Elizabeth, who like her was to bear a son in extraordinary circumstance. As she travelled towards the hills of Judaea to her cousin's home at Ain Karim, about five miles west of Jerusalem, her mind would almost certainly pick up another thread in her people's tradition.

The thought had been started up by the angel's words, 'The power of the Most High will cover you with its shadow'. The angel had used words which referred directly to the cloud in which the Israelites of old had seen God's presence upon earth. At Mount Sinai, when Moses received the Law, the glory of God had appeared in a cloud, which seemed like a devouring fire. On coming down from the mountain, Moses had built a tent according to the pattern revealed to him. This tent was to serve as a meeting place for the people, and a sanctuary for their God.

The ark of the covenant was the most precious piece of furniture in this tent, and the cloud of God's presence, the Shekinah, settled above the ark. When God wished the people to move on in the wilderness, the Shekinah rose from the ark, and the people were led on their journey by a cloud by day and a pillar of fire by night.

At a later date King David brought the ark up from the west to his own citadel of Zion, but the ark rested for three months at the home of Obed-edom. Finally, King Solomon built a temple in Jerusalem to house the ark and the presence of God. In later Jewish tradition the Shekinah came to be identified with the Wisdom of God, conceived as a second divine Person.

With the collapse of the kingdom of Judah and the destruction of the Temple by the Babylonians in 589 BC the glory of God seemed to have departed from Israel. The Temple was desecrated, the people taken off into captivity. The faith of Israel, however, not only remained, but was purified and strengthened. When the captives, or rather their offspring, returned home some seventy years later they set about rebuilding the Temple and reconstituting their national and religious life under the leadership of Ezra and Nehemiah.

Now the veneration of God's presence in their midst began to take on a fresh character. The devout among the Jews sensed that the Lord would come to dwell amongst his people in an even more significant way than he had done in the cloud above the ark of the covenant. The Temple and its worship was already becoming, in their eyes, more of a symbol than a reality. The devout who waited for the consolation of Israel were thinking more and more of the Messiah, the wonderful Saviour who was to come and redeem his people, as the prophets had foretold. His return would be the true return of the glory of God to Israel. This new, expectant mentality is expressed, for example, by the prophet Zephaniah:

> Shout for joy, daughter of Zion,
> Israel, shout aloud!
> Yahweh, the king of Israel, is in your midst;
> you have no more evil to fear.

Our Lady was steeped in the traditional belief in the presence of God in the Shekinah, and she was born into an atmosphere of expectancy of the final Messianic coming of God to his people. As she journeyed towards her cousin's home, the whole picture became clearer to her. The angel, she realized, had compared her to the ark of the covenant, the bearer of the Shekinah. He was telling her that she was to be the mother of the Wisdom of God. And now, as her journey progressed, this thought received dramatic confirmation. She was travelling through the hill country of Judaea; and as on that memorable journey of old when King David brought the ark of the covenant up to Jerusalem so she, the living ark of the new covenant, did not go directly to Jerusalem, but made a halt at about the same place where her cousin Elizabeth now lived.

It was here, in the happy atmosphere of family and a shared faith, that Mary received confirmation that she was the ark of the new covenant, for no sooner had Mary greeted her cousin than the babe in Elizabeth's womb leapt, just as David had leapt and danced before the ark of the covenant, and

Elizabeth, inspired by God, repeated anew the substance of the angel's greeting to Mary, adding these words: 'Why should I be honoured with a visit from the mother of my Lord?' – words which are parallel to those spoken by King David: 'However can the ark of Yahweh come to me?'

David had leapt before the ark of the covenant, which carried the Ten Words of God; the embryonic John the Baptist leapt before Mary, the ark of the new covenant, for she bore not just Ten Words of God, but the Word of God himself.

St Luke carries the parallelism between the two arks a little further in his postscript: Mary stayed with Elizabeth about three months, which was the length of time that the ark of the covenant of Yahweh had rested with the family of Obed-edom.

MARY VISITS HER KINSWOMAN ELIZABETH: LUKE 1.39–45, 56

Mary set out at that time and went as quickly as she could to a town in the hill country of Judah. She went into Zechariah's house and greeted Elizabeth. Now as soon as Elizabeth heard Mary's greeting, the child leapt in her womb and Elizabeth was filled with the Holy Spirit. She gave a loud cry and said, 'Of all women you are the most blessed, and blessed is the fruit of your womb. Why should I be honoured with a visit from the mother of my Lord? For the moment your greeting reached my ears, the child in my womb leapt for joy. Yes, blessed is she who believed that the promise made her by the Lord would be fulfilled.'

... Mary stayed with Elizabeth about three months and then went back home.

3

The Nativity

David is anointed: 1 Samuel 16.1–13

Yahweh said to Samuel, 'How long will you go on mourning over Saul when I have rejected him as king of Israel? Fill your horn with oil and go. I am sending you to Jesse of Bethlehem, for I have chosen myself a king among his sons.' Samuel replied, 'How can I go? When Saul hears of it he will kill me.' Then Yahweh said, 'Take a heifer with you and say, "I have come to sacrifice to Yahweh". Invite Jesse to the sacrifice, and then I myself will tell you what you must do; you must anoint to me the one I point out to you.'

Samuel did what Yahweh ordered and went to Bethlehem. The elders of the town came trembling to meet him and asked, 'Seer, have you come with good intentions towards us?' 'Yes,' he replied 'I have come to sacrifice to Yahweh. Purify yourselves and come with me to the sacrifice.' He purified Jesse and his sons and invited them to the sacrifice.

When he arrived, he caught sight of Eliab and thought, 'Surely Yahweh's anointed one stands there before him', but Yahweh said to Samuel, 'Take no notice of his appearance or his height for I have rejected him; God does not see as man sees; man looks at appearances but Yahweh looks at the heart'. Jesse then called Abinadab and presented him to Samuel, who said, 'Yahweh has not chosen this one either' ... Jesse presented his seven sons to Samuel, but Samuel said to Jesse, 'Yahweh has not chosen these'. He then asked Jesse, 'Are these all the sons you have?' He answered, 'There is still one left, the youngest; he is out looking after the sheep'. Then Samuel said to Jesse, 'Send for him; we will not sit down to eat until he comes'. Jesse had him sent for, a boy of fresh complexion, with fine eyes and pleasant bearing. Yahweh said, 'Come, anoint him, for this is the one'. At this, Samuel took the horn of oil and anointed him where he stood with his brothers; and the spirit of Yahweh seized on David and stayed with him from that day on. As for Samuel, he rose and went to Ramah.

David's prayer: 2 Samuel 7.18–29

King David then went in and, seated before Yahweh, said:

'Who am I, Lord Yahweh, and what is my House, that you have led me as far as this? Yet in your sight, Lord Yahweh, this is still not far enough, and you make your promises extend to the House of your servant for a far-distant future. What more can David say to you, when you yourself have singled out your servant, Lord Yahweh? For your servant's sake, this dog of yours, you have done so great a thing by revealing this to your servant. In this is your greatness, Lord Yahweh; there is none like you, no God but you alone, as our own ears have heard. Is there another people on the earth like your people Israel, with a God setting out to redeem them and make them his people, make them renowned, work great and terrible things on their behalf, drive nations out and gods before his people? You have constituted your people Israel to be your own people for ever; and you, Yahweh, have become their God. Now, Lord Yahweh, always keep the promise you have made your servant and his House, and do as you have said. Your name will be exalted for ever and men will say, "Yahweh Sabaoth is God over Israel." The House of your servant David will be made secure in your presence, since you yourself, Yahweh Sabaoth, God of Israel, have made this revelation to your servant, "I will build you a House"; hence your servant has ventured to offer this prayer to you. Yes, Lord Yahweh, you are God indeed, your words are true and you have made this fair promise to your servant. Be pleased, then, to bless the House of your servant, that it may continue for ever in your presence; for you, Lord Yahweh, have spoken; and with your blessing the House of your servant will be for ever blessed.'

The Messiah–King: Isaiah 11.1–9
A shoot springs from the stock of Jesse,
a scion thrusts from his roots:
on him the spirit of Yahweh rests,
a spirit of wisdom and insight,
a spirit of counsel and power,
a spirit of knowledge and of the fear of Yahweh.
(The fear of Yahweh is his breath.)
He does not judge by appearances,
he gives no verdict on hearsay,
but judges the wretched with integrity,
and with equity gives a verdict for the poor of the land.
His word is a rod that strikes the ruthless,
his sentences bring death to the wicked.

Integrity is the loincloth round his waist,
faithfulness the belt about his hips.

The dynasty of David: Micah 5.1
But you, (Bethlehem) Ephrathah,
the least of the clans of Judah,
out of you will be born for me
the one who is to rule over Israel;
his origin goes back to the distant past,
to the days of old.

'God is with us': Isaiah 7.13–14
[Yahweh spoke to Ahaz through the prophet Isaiah]:
   Listen now, House of David:
   are you not satisfied with trying the patience of men
   without trying the patience of my God, too?
   The Lord himself, therefore,
   will give you a sign.
   It is this: the maiden is with child
   and will soon give birth to a son
   whom she will call Immanuel.

MEDITATION

At Christmas time we love to sing hymns and carols in which the shepherds and their flocks figure prominently. But do we realize that this pastoral setting, which forms the background to the story of the manifestation of the Word made flesh in the birth of Jesus, is much more than a bit of local, decorative colour? St Luke tells of the shepherds and their flocks for a specific theological reason. He is recalling the day at Bethlehem when David was called from minding his father's sheep, and was anointed by Samuel to be king of Israel. By mentioning Bethlehem, the shepherds, and Joseph, who was of David's line, St Luke is declaring that God has fulfilled his promise, that David's dynasty would endure for ever, and that from this dynasty would come the Messiah–King.

St Matthew too tells us that Jesus was born in Bethlehem, and quotes a prophecy from the book of Micah, which speaks of the leader who will be born there, and 'who will shepherd my people Israel'. In place of the adoration of the shepherds, however, St Matthew has the story of the visit of the three non-Jewish kings from the east. These men represented the whole human race, and revealed the fulfilment of another prophecy of Isaiah:

> the riches of the sea will flow to you,
> the wealth of the nations come to you;
>
> camels in throngs will cover you,
> and dromedaries of Midian and Ephah;

everyone in Sheba will come,
bringing gold and incense
and singing the praise of Yahweh.
(Isaiah 60.5–6)

The story has been rounded off. The promise to Abraham has been fulfilled: all the nations of the earth have been blessed in his posterity; the promise to David has likewise been fulfilled: the Messiah–King has been born from his dynasty; and the Wisdom of God, who guided the Israelites through the wilderness into the Promised Land, and came to rest in the Shekinah above the ark of the covenant within the Holy of Holies in the Temple, has finally descended to earth, becoming flesh and blood in the womb of the virgin Mary, and being born of her and laid in a crib at Bethlehem. All the strands of the Old Testament expectation converge in the Babe of Bethlehem, and we come to the fundamental mystery of the Christian faith, a mystery which Isaiah glimpsed long before when he gave the Messiah the supreme title of Immanuel, 'God with us'. We underline the importance of this mystery by bowing our heads as we recite these words in the Creed: 'was incarnate of the virgin Mary by the power of the Holy Spirit, and was made man.'

Our Lady, we are told by St Luke, stored up in her heart all of the events in her Son's life; the birth of her son must have been for her, as it is for us, the deepest mystery of all. Our Lady, as no one else could ever be, was aware of the paradox that here was one who was both God and man. The angel had told her that the child born to her would be the Son of the Most High, and had alluded to the Shekinah above the ark of the covenant, so that she would know what he meant when he said, 'The power of the Most High will cover you with its shadow'. And she believed the angel. As Elizabeth commented: 'Blessed is she who believed that the promise made to her by the Lord would be fulfilled.' At the same time she knew, as no one else ever could, that he was truly her baby, her flesh and blood.

The New Testament writers take up this same theme in

the way they present the story of our Lord's life. The evangelists are at pains to declare that Jesus is Lord, that he is no less than God himself. St John puts it quite explicitly when he reports our Lord's saying: 'The Father and I are one', and 'Before Abraham ever was, I am'. The miracles, too, are not just impressive wonders but signs of divinity, of the power to give life, something which belongs to God alone; and he often performed the miracle on the Sabbath, precisely because that was the day consecrated to God. As he said when challenged: 'My Father works on this day, and so do I.' In association with another miracle, he pointed out that he did it to demonstrate that he had power to forgive sins, the prerogative of God. Calming a storm was likewise considered an activity reserved to the Creator.

But this open declaration of our Lord's divinity by the evangelists never causes them to obscure his humanity. The Gospels present a picture of a real man who ate and slept and even wept. And at the end, his humanity is all too convincingly revealed in his slow and agonized death. The New Testament tells us plainly that Jesus Christ is true God and true man.

The doctrinal history of the Church in the first few centuries is the story of how the faithful fought to maintain the integrity of this mystery. In an attempt to release the tension of this paradox and reduce the mystery to terms comprehensible to the mind of man, now one side and now the other was denied. Some said that Jesus was the Son of God only in a metaphorical sense, that he merely had some kind of perfect relationship with God. Others said that he was truly God, and his manhood merely a disguise, that he made use of the appearance of a human body, but was not fully man. In face of these contrasting errors the Church maintained, on the one hand, that mankind could only be redeemed by one who was truly God, and on the other hand, that anything in our human nature that had not been assumed by the Word of God could not have been redeemed. The Church was never able to explain this mystery, but resolutely preserved it intact, thus handing on

for all generations the experience of Mary who knew that
the child in her arms was her child, but knew also, by faith,
that he was the Son of God.

The fourth ecumenical council of the Church, which met
at Chalcedon in the year 451, defined how we should speak
about our Lord Jesus Christ so as to deny neither his divinity nor his humanity. This statement is not an explanation of
the mystery. It merely keeps us on the right track in which
we may contemplate the mystery of the incarnation and so
find nourishment for our souls.

> Therefore, following the holy Fathers, we all with one
> accord teach men to acknowledge one and the same Son,
> our Lord Jesus Christ, at once complete in manhood, truly
> God and truly man, consisting also of a reasonable soul
> and body; of one substance with the Father as regards his
> Godhead, and at the same time of one substance with us
> as regards his manhood; like us in all respects, apart from
> sin; as regards his Godhead, begotten of the Father before
> the ages, but yet as regards his manhood begotten, for us
> men and for our salvation, of Mary the Virgin, the God-
> bearer.

In making this dogmatic statement, the Fathers of Chalcedon
were simply expanding what St Paul had said in essence in
the very opening verses of his letter to the Romans:

> This news is about the Son of God who, according to the
> human nature he took, was a descendant of David: it is
> about Jesus Christ our Lord who, in the order of the
> spirit, the spirit of holiness that was in him, was
> proclaimed Son of God in all his power through his resur-
> rection from the dead. (Romans 1.3–5)

CHRIST, THE REDEEMER, IS BORN:
LUKE 2.1–20

Now at this time Caesar Augustus issued a decree for a census of the whole world to be taken. This census – the first – took place while Quirinius was governor of Syria, and everyone went to his own town to be registered. So Joseph set out from the town of Nazareth in Galilee and travelled up to Judaea, to the town of David called Bethlehem, since he was of David's House and line, in order to be registered together with Mary, his betrothed, who was with child. While they were there the time came for her to have her child, and she gave birth to a son, her first-born. She wrapped him in swaddling clothes, and laid him in a manger because there was no room for them at the inn. In the countryside close by there were shepherds who lived in the fields and took it in turns to watch their flocks during the night. The angel of the Lord appeared to them and the glory of the Lord shone round them. They were terrified, but the angel said, 'Do not be afraid. Listen, I bring you news of great joy, a joy to be shared by the whole people. Today in the town of David a saviour has been born to you; he is Christ the Lord. And here is a sign for you; you will find a baby wrapped in swaddling clothes and lying in a manger.' And suddenly there was with the angel a great throng of the heavenly host, praising God and singing:

'Glory to God in the highest heaven, and peace to men who enjoy his favour'.

Now when the angels had gone from them into heaven, the shepherds said to one another, 'Let us go to Bethlehem and see this thing that has happened which the Lord has made known to us'. So they hurried away and found Mary and Joseph, and the baby lying in the manger. When they saw the child they repeated what they had been told about him, and everyone who heard it was astonished at what the shepherds had to say. As for Mary, she treasured all these things and pondered them in her heart. And the shepherds went back glorifying and praising God for all they had heard and seen; it was exactly as they had been told.

4

The Presentation

The anointing of the Temple: Daniel 9.20–4
I was still speaking, still at prayer, confessing my own sins
and the sins of my people Israel and placing my plea
before Yahweh my God for the holy mountain of my God,
still speaking, still at prayer, when Gabriel, the being I
had seen originally in a vision, flew suddenly down to me
at the hour of the evening sacrifice. He said to me,
'Daniel, you see me; I have come down to teach you how
to understand. When your pleading began, a word was
uttered, and I have come to tell you what it is. You are a
man specially chosen. Grasp the meaning of the word,
understand the vision:

> 'Seventy weeks are decreed
> for your people and your holy city,
> for putting an end to transgression,
> for placing the seals on sin,
> for expiating crime,
> for introducing everlasting integrity,
> for setting the seal on vision and on prophecy,
> for anointing the Holy of Holies.'

The redemption of the first-born: Exodus 13.11–15
'When Yahweh brings you to the land of the Canaanites –
as he swore to you and your fathers he would do – and
gives it to you, you are to make over to Yahweh all that

first issues from the womb, and every first-born cast by
your animals: these males belong to Yahweh. But every
first-born donkey you will redeem with an animal from
your flocks. If you do not redeem it, you must break its
neck. Of your sons, every first-born of men must be
redeemed. And when your son asks you in days to come,
"What does this mean?" you will tell him, "By sheer power
Yahweh brought us out of Egypt, out of the house of
slavery. When Pharaoh stubbornly refused to let us go,
Yahweh killed all the first-born in the land of Egypt, of
man and beast alike. For this I sacrifice to Yahweh every
male that first issues from the womb, and redeem every
first-born of my sons.'"

The Lord will come to his Temple: Malachi 3.1–4
Look, I am going to send my messenger to prepare a way
before me And the Lord you are seeking will suddenly
enter his Temple; and the angel of the covenant whom
you are longing for, yes, he is coming, says Yahweh
Sabaoth. Who will be able to resist the day of his coming?
Who will remain standing when he appears? For he is like
the refiner's fire and the fullers' alkali. He will take his
seat as refiner and purifier; he will purify the sons of Levi
and refine them like gold and silver, and then they will
make the offering to Yahweh as it should be made.

The Light of the Nations: Isaiah 49.1–6
   Islands, listen to me,
   pay attention, remotest peoples.
   Yahweh called me before I was born,
   from my mother's womb he pronounced my name.

   He made my mouth a sharp sword,
   and hid me in the shadow of his hand.
   He made me into a sharpened arrow,
   and concealed me in his quiver.

   He said to me, 'You are my servant (Israel)
   in whom I shall be glorified';

while I was thinking, 'I have toiled in vain,
I have exhausted myself for nothing';

and all the while my cause was with Yahweh,
my reward with my God.
I was honoured in the eyes of Yahweh,
my God was my strength.

And now Yahweh has spoken,
he who formed me in the womb to be his servant,
to bring Jacob back to him,
to gather Israel to him:

'It is not enough for you to be my servant,
to restore the tribes of Jacob and bring back the
    survivors of Israel;
I will make you the light of the nations
so that my salvation may reach the ends of the earth'.

God in his Temple: **Psalm 48.9–14**

God, in your Temple
    we reflect on your love:
God, your praise, like your name,
    reaches to the ends of the world.

Your right hand holds the victory;
    Mount Zion rejoices,
the daughters of Judah exult
    to have your rulings.

Go through Zion, walk round her,
    counting her towers,
admiring her walls,
    reviewing her palaces;

then tell the next generation
    that God is here,
our God and leader,
    for ever and ever.

MEDITATION

The prophet Daniel was at prayer at the hour of the evening sacrifice, when the angel Gabriel appeared to him, bringing a message from God. The prophet was distressed by the plight of his people, for he lived at a time when vicious persecution raged against them. He asked for a sign to tell him when this would all end, when deliverance would come and the sanctuary of God once again be made holy.

The seventy weeks could be understood as a reference to the period of seventy years, from the year 605 BC when Jeremiah first prophesied that the exiles would return, until their return and the rebuilding of the Temple; or it could be understood as more or less seventy Sabbatical periods (seven times seventy years) beginning with the same year and running on until the consecration of the Temple by Judas Maccabeus in 164 BC. Early Christian writers saw in Daniel's vision a dim foreshadowing of the consecration of the Temple by our Lord when he was presented there by Mary and Joseph.

The narrative of our Lord's birth is prefaced by an account of another vision. We find Zechariah kneeling, like Daniel, before the divine presence. He is told by the same angel Gabriel that he will father a son who will be the forerunner of the one who is to deliver his people, and indeed all people, from the distress which afflicts mankind. At last the anointed one is to come who will consecrate not just the Jerusalem Temple but mankind: who will become, through their anointing by the Holy Spirit, the body of Christ and hence the true Temple of God. The coming of this son promised to Zechariah had also been prophesied in Old Testament times. The angel Gabriel made clear to Zechariah that the oracle of Malachi, which links the expectation of the forerunner with that of the Lord coming to his Temple, had been fulfilled.

The account of the Presentation of the infant Jesus in the Temple at Jerusalem introduces a new element: we are given a hint of the means whereby this Lord of the Temple is going to accomplish the salvation, the anointing, of mankind. We are told that Mary and Joseph faithfully carried out all the prescriptions of the Law concerning the birth of a first-born son. First of all, eight days after his birth, they had the child circumcised. A mere drop of the infant's blood was shed; by this symbolic act he was shown to be truly of the seed of Abraham, and therefore true man. Then in the Presentation scene, forty days after his birth, our Lady came to the Temple for the ceremony of her purification, and offered the sacrifice of the poor, a pair of turtle doves and two young pigeons. Had they been wealthy, a lamb would have been offered as the redemption price for the child, but as they were poor a pair of turtle doves sufficed.

But there is irony latent in Luke's concise statement, for although the redemption price was paid for the infant Jesus, as things turn out in the end, it was he who became the redemption price paid for the whole of mankind; he is the ram caught in the thicket who was sacrificed in place of Abraham's son, Isaac.

The Servant of the Lord of whom Isaiah sang, was to be not only a light to enlighten every nation, but a suffering servant. The anointing of the Holy of Holies would be performed in the blood of him who was no less than Lord of the Temple.

Finally this theme of sacrifice is taken up quite explicitly, although enigmatically, by the prophet Simeon. Simeon looks upon the child, and takes up the strain of Isaiah's prophecy, hailing the child as the glory of Israel and the light of all nations. Then, turning to Mary, he proclaims that her child will lead to a crisis among his people: some will see him and believe, others will look upon him with blind eyes and reject him, thus calling down judgement upon themselves. Simeon's brief comment reminds us of our Lord's own sayings as recorded by St John:

> 'On these grounds is sentence pronounced:
> that though the light has come into the world
> men have shown they prefer
> darkness to the light
> because their deeds were evil'. (John 3.19)

> 'It is for judgement
> that I have come into this world,
> so that those without sight may see
> and those with sight turn blind'. (John 9.39)

And so the prophet Simeon, speaking of the rejection of Christ, picks up the theme of sacrifice that is latent in St Luke's narrative; he foretells the ultimate rejection of this child, of his meek acceptance of his role as sacrificial lamb upon the cross.

Simeon's last word is addressed to Mary. Here, as so often, there are subtle overtones from the Old Testament which give us a clue to the meaning of what is being said. In the second servant song of Isaiah, which contains the reference to the 'light of the nations', we read:

> 'Yahweh called me before I was born,
> from my mother's womb he pronounced my name.

> 'He made my mouth a sharp sword,
> and hid me in the shadow of his hand'. (Isaiah 49.1–2)

Was Simeon thinking of the child, whose very nature and function was to precipitate crisis, as though the child were cutting into the very being of his own mother? Part of what is meant by a sword piercing Mary's soul is that the people of Israel, whom Mary, the Daughter of Israel, personifies, will be split into two factions: those who accept her Son and those who reject him. In times to come that same division appeared in the whole of humanity.

Whatever the full explanation of the sequence of thoughts in Simeon's mind, his saying is most meaningfully related to the sacrificial scene at Calvary. There, Mary, beholding her Son, felt his agony in her own soul; and, standing at the foot of the cross, she became representative of the whole body of Christ. We too, the Church, are called to enter into his sufferings, to 'make up what is lacking in the sufferings of Christ, for the sake of his body, which is the Church' (Colossians 1.24). Thus in her union with the passion of her Son she revealed what would become manifested in the hearts of men and women down the ages.

THE INFANT JESUS IS PRESENTED IN THE TEMPLE: LUKE 2.22–35

*And when the day came for them to be purified
as laid down by the Law of Moses, they took
him up to Jerusalem to present him to the Lord
– observing what stands written in the Law of
the Lord:* Every first-born male must be
consecrated to the Lord – *and also to offer
in sacrifice, in accordance with what is said in
the Law of the Lord,* a pair of turtledoves or
two young pigeons. *Now in Jerusalem there
was a man named Simeon. He was an upright
and devout man; he looked forward to Israel's
comforting and the Holy Spirit rested on him.
It had been revealed to him by the Holy Spirit
that he would not see death until he had set
eyes on the Christ of the Lord. Prompted by the
Spirit he came to the Temple; and when the
parents brought in the child Jesus to do for him
what the Law required, he took him into his
arms and blessed God; and he said:*

'*Now, Master, you can let your servant go in
peace,
just as you promised;*

because my eyes have seen the salvation
which you have prepared for all nations to see,
a light to enlighten the pagans
and the glory of your people Israel'.

As the child's father and mother stood there
wondering at the things that were being said
about him, Simeon blessed them and said to
Mary his mother, 'You see this child: he is
destined for the fall and for the rising of many
in Israel, destined to be a sign that is rejected —
and a sword will pierce your own soul too — so
that the secret thoughts of many may be laid
bare'.

5

The Finding in the Temple

The Passover: Deuteronomy 16.1–8
Observe the month of Abib and celebrate the Passover for Yahweh your God, because it was in the month of Abib that Yahweh your God brought you out of Egypt by night. You must sacrifice a passover from your flock or herd for Yahweh your God in the place where Yahweh chooses to give his name a home. You must not eat leavened bread with this; for seven days you must eat it with unleavened bread, the bread of emergency, for it was in great haste that you came out of the land of Egypt; so you will remember, all the days of your life, the day you came out of the land of Egypt. For seven days no leaven must be found in any house throughout your territory, nor must any of the meat that you sacrifice in the evening of the first day be kept overnight until morning. You may not sacrifice the passover in any of the towns that Yahweh your God gives you; but only in the place where Yahweh your God chooses to give his name a home, there you must sacrifice the passover, in the evening at sunset, at the hour at which you came out of Egypt. You must cook it and eat it in the place Yahweh your God chooses, and in the morning you are to return and go to your tents. For six days you shall eat unleavened bread; on the seventh day there shall be an assembly for Yahweh your God; and you must do no work.

The dedication of Samuel: 1 Samuel 1.19–28
They rose early in the morning and worshipped before Yahweh and then set out and returned to their home in Ramah. Elkanah had intercourse with Hannah his wife and Yahweh was mindful of her. She conceived and gave birth to a son, and called him Samuel 'since' she said 'I asked Yahweh for him.'

When a year had gone by, the husband Elkanah went up again with all his family to offer the annual sacrifice to Yahweh and to fulfil his vow. Hannah, however, did not go up, having said to her husband, 'Not before the child is weaned. Then I will bring him and present him before Yahweh and he shall stay there for ever.' Elkanah her husband then said to her, 'Do what you think fit; wait until you have weaned him. May Yahweh bring about what you have said.' So the woman stayed behind and nursed her child until his weaning.

When she had weaned him, she took him up with her together with a three-year old bull, an ephah of flour and a skin of wine, and she brought him to the temple of Yahweh at Shiloh; and the child was with them. They slaughtered the bull and the child's mother came to Eli. She said, 'If you please, my lord. As you live, my lord, I am the woman who stood here beside you, praying to Yahweh. This is the child I prayed for, and Yahweh granted me what I asked him. Now I make him over to Yahweh for the whole of his life. He is made over to Yahweh.'

There she left him, for Yahweh.

The glory of God fills the Temple: Isaiah 6.1–5
In the year of King Uzziah's death I saw the Lord Yahweh seated on a high throne; his train filled the sanctuary; above him stood seraphs, each one with six wings: two to cover its face, two to cover its feet and two for flying.

And they cried out to one another in this way,

> 'Holy, holy, holy is Yahweh Sabaoth.
> His glory fills the whole earth.'

The foundations of the threshold shook with the voice of the one who cried out, and the Temple was filled with smoke. I said:

'What a wretched state I am in! I am lost,
for I am a man of unclean lips
and I live among a people of unclean lips,
and my eyes have looked at the King, Yahweh Sabaoth.'

The rewards of Wisdom: Proverbs 3.13–20
Happy the man who discovers wisdom,
    the man who gains discernment:
gaining her is more rewarding than silver,
    more profitable than gold.
She is beyond the price of pearls,
    nothing you could covet is her equal.
In her right hand is length of days;
    in her left hand, riches and honour.
Her ways are delightful ways,
    her paths all lead to contentment.
She is a tree of life for those who hold her fast,
    those who cling to her live happy lives.

By wisdom, Yahweh set the earth on its foundations,
    by discernment, he fixed the heavens firm.
Through his knowledge the depths were carved out,
    and the clouds rain down the dew.

I come to do your will: Psalm 40.6–9
You, who wanted no sacrifice or oblation,
    opened my ear,
you asked no holocaust or sacrifice for sin;
    then I said, 'Here I am! I am coming!'

In the scroll of the book am I not commanded
    to obey your will?
My God, I have always loved your Law
    from the depths of my being.

I have always proclaimed the righteousness of Yahweh
in the Great Assembly;
nor do I mean to stop proclaiming,
as you know well.

MEDITATION

The first section of St Luke's Gospel (chapters 1 and 2) ends with an account of that phase in our Lord's life when he was passing from childhood to the acceptance of adult responsibility in the Jewish community. For the young Jew this transition took place at the age of twelve, and was marked by his first attendance at the feast of the Passover in Jerusalem. As in the previous scene, the thought of sacrifice is in the background, for the Temple was the place of sacrifice. There was, however, a sacrificial feast which, although it was initiated in the Temple, was celebrated in the homes of the people. That feast was the Passover, and it was on the occasion of his first celebration of the Passover that Jesus was lost and then found in the Temple.

In origin this festival was connected with the sacrifice of the first fruits of the flock, and the ceremony began with the sacrifice of the paschal lamb. This sacrifice had, however, become attached to the decisive national historical event, the deliverance of the Israelites out of Egypt. The Passover was thus primarily the commemoration of the salvation of the people of Israel. The second part of the Passover feast was also a commemoration of that night when the Israelites had eaten a hasty meal of unleavened bread as they were about to escape out of Egypt.

In the gospel episode we now consider, our Lord had begun to accept his vocation as an adult Jew; but in the eyes of St Luke he was presenting himself in the Temple as the new paschal lamb, by whose sacrifice, not only the Jews, but the whole human race would be redeemed. We see also a foreshadowing of the new Passover meal which, in due course, he was to institute as a memorial and representation of his redemptive sacrifice on the cross.

Commenting upon Exodus 12.1–20, which describes the Jewish Passover, the Jerusalem Bible has a most instructive footnote:

> The Jewish Passover hence becomes a rehearsal for the Christian Passover: the Lamb of God, Christ, is sacrificed (the cross) and eaten (the Last Supper) within the framework of the Jewish Passover (the first Holy Week). Thus he brings salvation to the world; and the mystical re-enactment of this redemptive act becomes the central feature of the Christian liturgy, organised round the Mass which is at once sacrifice and sacrificial meal.

The presence of Jesus in the Temple, as an infant and again when he was twelve years old, sets him in relation not only to the Passover, but to the Day of Atonement and to the whole system of Temple worship. The sacrifices of the Temple had been a means of preparing men for the perfect worship that Christ would inaugurate. With his coming these had served their purpose, and were to be superseded by the offering of the body of Christ. Chapters 7 to 10 of the Letter to the Hebrews contains a dissertation on the perfect sacrifice of Christ. There we read that 'He is abolishing the first sort (of sacrifice) to replace it with the second.' And the purpose of this is 'for us to be made holy by the offering of his body made once and for all in Jesus Christ.' In this new order of worship Christ is everything: victim, high priest, and the Temple of God in this world. As our great high priest he has entered into the heavenly temple and leads us into the presence of our eternal Father.

The Presentation and the Finding of Jesus in the Temple thus link up with other passages in the New Testament where the Temple is mentioned. There is the occasion when Jesus drove the money-changers out of the Temple, thereby declaring the inadequacy of the Jewish ritual, when he justified his action by saying, 'Destroy this sanctuary, and in three days I will raise it up'. By this he meant that the temple of his body would supply what the Jewish Temple could not, namely, a way of communication between God the Father and all mankind. And there is the very important incident at the well of Sychar when Jesus told the Samaritan woman that the day was coming when men would worship God neither upon Mount Gerizim nor upon Mount Zion, but in Spirit and in truth, that is, in him who is the new Mount Zion, the new Jerusalem, the new Temple.

It is against the background of Jesus as the true Temple that we must interpret the end of this scene when Mary and Joseph, after three days' searching, found Jesus talking with the teachers in the Temple. St Luke is not trying to comment on the psychology or ethics of family life, and is not describing an incident typical of parent–adolescent tension. He is continuing his teaching about the nature of Christ and his vocation. St Luke is also, in a veiled manner, alluding to the time when Jesus will after three days be found not amongst his earthly relations and disciples but in the company of his Father in heaven. His being found in the Temple after his first Passover is thus a foreshadowing of his Resurrection.

It is true that Jesus' immediate reply implies that his mother and foster-father had no real need to feel anxiety over him. But why? Because of who he was. His whole life was to be one of complete dedication to his Father. As the child Samuel had spent his whole life since babyhood in the service of the Temple, away from his natural home, while his mother came up and down each year with clothing for him, so Jesus' normal place of residence was away from home, in his Father's house, symbolized here by his remaining in the Temple, while Mary and Joseph set off for home; but as his subsequent return to Nazareth indicates, pursuit of his Father's affairs was not a matter of remaining in the Temple at Jerusalem either. The Wisdom of God dwelt fully in him, so that wherever he was, there he was busied about his Father's affairs. When Jesus asked: 'Did you not know that I must be busy with my Father's affairs?' he was not trying to justify his action, but inviting his people Israel, represented by Mary and Joseph, to ponder on who he was and what he had been called to do. In that question we might even detect a hint of his more anguished exclamation when he caught sight of Jerusalem and its Temple as he approached them for the last time: 'If you in your turn had only understood this day the message of peace!'

This appeal of our Lord to his people for their understanding and faith points to the final element in the concept of Christ as the true Temple of God upon earth. This new Temple must be filled with worshippers. By God's presence on earth we mean primarily his Son, born of the virgin Mary, dying upon the cross and rising from the dead, continuing sacramentally in his eucharistic body and blood, by which he makes present his sacrifice day by day and feeds his people who in turn, through the Holy Spirit, are built up into the real and ever-present temple of God upon earth. St Paul says: 'That is what we are – the temple of the living God' (2 Cor. 6.16). As in the pictures in the apses of ancient churches, the Good Shepherd never appears unless surrounded by his sheep. The ultimate mystery and joy of the presence of God with us is that, as in the vision of Isaiah, his train fills the temple. His holiness flows truly into us. Christ has 'offered himself as the perfect sacrifice to God' so that 'we can purify our inner self from dead actions so that we do our service to the living God.' His sacrifice has been effective as the sacrifices under the old covenant could never be. 'By virtue of that one single offering he has achieved the eternal perfection of all whom he is sanctifying.' And so God's people join in the declaration from Psalm 40, put by the writer of the Letter to the Hebrews into the mouth of Christ:

> You who wanted no sacrifice or oblation,
> prepared a body for me.
> You took no pleasure in holocausts or sacrifices for sin;
> then I said,
> . . .
> 'God, here I am! I am coming to obey your will'.
>
> (Hebrews 10.6–7)

IN THE TEMPLE, ASKING AND ANSWERING QUESTIONS: LUKE 2.41–52

Every year his parents used to go to Jerusalem for the feast of the Passover. When he was twelve years old, they went up for the feast as usual. When they were on their way home after the feast, the boy Jesus stayed behind in Jerusalem without his parents knowing it. They assumed he was with the caravan, and it was only after a day's journey that they went to look for him among their relations and acquaintances. When they failed to find him they went back to Jerusalem looking for him everywhere.

Three days later, they found him in the Temple, sitting among the doctors, listening to them, and asking them questions; and all those who heard him were astounded at his intelligence and his replies. They were overcome when they saw him, and his mother said to him, 'My child, why have you done this to us? See how worried your father and I have been, looking for you.' 'Why were you looking for me?' he replied 'Did you not know that I must

*be busy with my Father's affairs?' But they did
not understand what he meant.*

*He then went down with them and came to
Nazareth and lived under their authority. His
mother stored up all these things in her heart.
And Jesus increased in wisdom, in stature, and
in favour with God and men.*

PART TWO

The Mysteries of Light

1

The Baptism in the Jordan

Water and light: Genesis 1.1–5
In the beginning God created the heavens and the earth.
Now the earth was a formless void, there was darkness
over the deep, and God's spirit hovered over the water.

God said, 'Let there be light', and there was light. God
saw that light was good, and God divided light from
darkness. God called light 'day', and darkness he called
'night'. Evening came and morning came : the first day.

The true light – the Word: John 1.1–9
    In the beginning was the Word:
    the Word was with God
    and the Word was God.
    He was with God in the beginning.
    Through him all things came to be,
    not one thing had its being but through him.
    All that came to be had life in him
    and that life was the light of men,
    a light that shines in the dark,
    a light that darkness could not overpower.

    A man came, sent by God.
    His name was John.
    He came as a witness,

as a witness to speak for the light,
so that everyone might believe through him.
He was not the light,
only a witness to speak for the light.

The Word was the true light
that enlightens all men.

The water of judgement: Genesis 6.13, 17–22
God said to Noah, 'The end has come for all things of
flesh; I have decided this, because the earth is full of
violence of man's making, and I will efface them from the
earth.

. . .

'For my part I mean to bring a flood, and send the
waters over the earth, to destroy all flesh on it, every
living creature under heaven; everything on earth shall
perish. But I will establish my Covenant with you, and
you must go on board the ark, yourself, your sons, your
wife, and your sons' wives along with you. From all living
creatures, from all flesh, you must take two of each kind
aboard the ark, to save their lives with yours; they must be
a male and a female. Of every kind of bird, of every kind
of animal and of every kind of reptile on the ground, two
must go with you so that their lives may be saved. For
your part provide yourself with eatables of all kinds, and
lay in a store of them, to serve as food for yourself and
them.' Noah did this; he did all that God had ordered
him.

Water and life: Ezekiel 47.1–12
He brought me back to the entrance of the Temple,
where a stream came out from under the Temple threshold and flowed eastwards, since the Temple faced east.
The water flowed from under the right side of the
Temple, south of the altar. He took me out by the north
gate and led me right round outside as far as the outer
east gate where the water flowed out on the right-hand

side. The man went to the east holding his measuring line and measured off a thousand cubits; he then made me wade across the stream; the water reached my ankles. He measured off another thousand and made me wade across the stream again; the water reached my knees. He measured off another thousand and made me wade across again; the water reached my waist. He measured off another thousand; it was now a river which I could not cross; the stream had swollen and was now deep water, a river impossible to cross. He then said, 'Do you see, son of man? He took me further, then brought me back to the bank of the river. When I got back, there were many trees on each bank of the river. He said, 'This water flows east down to the Arabah and to the sea; and flowing into the sea it makes its waters wholesome. Wherever the river flows, all living creatures teeming in it will live. Fish will be very plentiful, for wherever the water goes it brings health, and life teems wherever the river flows. There will be fishermen on its banks. Fishing nets will be spread from En-gedi to En-eglaim. The fish will be as varied and as plentiful as the fish of the Great Sea. The marshes and lagoons, however, will not become wholesome, but will remain salt. Along the river, on either bank, will grow every kind of fruit tree with leaves that never wither and fruit that never fails; they will bear fruit every month, because this water comes from the sanctuary. And their fruit will be good to eat and the leaves medicinal.

Light and life for ever: Revelation 21.22 – 22.5
I saw there was no temple in the city since the Lord God Almighty and the Lamb were themselves the temple, and the city did not need the sun or the moon for light, since it was lit by the radiant glory of God and the Lamb was a lighted torch for it. The pagan nations will live by its light and the kings of the earth will bring it their treasures. The gates of it will never be shut by day – and there will be no night there – and the nations will come, bringing their treasure and their wealth. Nothing unclean may come

into it: no one who does what is loathsome or false, but only those who are listed in the Lamb's book of life.

Then the angel showed me the river of life, rising from the throne of God and of the Lamb and flowing crystal-clear down the middle of the city street. On either side of the river were the trees of life, which bear twelve crops of fruit in a year, one in each month, and the leaves of which are the cure for the pagans.

The ban will be lifted. The throne of God and of the Lamb will be in its place in the city; his servants will worship him, they will see him face to face, and his name will be written on their foreheads. It will never be night again and they will not need lamplight or sunlight, because the Lord God will be shining on them. They will reign for ever and ever.

MEDITATION

How appropriate that the first of the Mysteries of Light is the Baptism of Jesus in the Jordan! The Gospels tell us that on the first day of his public ministry Jesus let himself be immersed in water; and the book of Genesis tells us that in the prelude to creation 'God's Spirit hovered over the water.' Then, so that from this fundamental element, as a kind of matrix, all specific being should be born, God spoke and energy was created. 'God said, "Let there be light", and there was light.' The poem continues, telling how all particular beings were formed successively, as though the product of a week's work by a master-craftsman. In the record of the history of salvation as recorded in Holy Scripture the themes of water and of light remain closely connected.

Water is life, and in the Holy Scriptures water features predominantly as a symbol of spiritual or supernatural life. In Psalm 1 the virtuous man is described as one who is

> like a tree that is planted
> by water streams,
> yielding its fruit in season,
> its leaves never fading;
> success attends all he does.

In Psalm 42 God himself is likened to a source of water, and the devout man or woman is one who thirsts for this divine water.

As a doe longs
for running streams,
so longs my soul
for you, my God.
My soul thirsts for God,
the God of life;
when shall I go to see
the face of God?

Here thirst for God (water) is linked with the desire to see God (light). Our Lord Jesus made full use of this ancient symbolism. On the last day of the great festival of Tabernacles, a festival during which the water-miracles of Moses were commemorated in prayers for rain, Jesus cried out, 'If any man is thirsty, let him come to me! Let the man come and drink who believes in me!' (John 7.37–8). Similarly during his encounter with the woman of Samaria who had come to draw water from Jacob's well, and from whom he had asked for a drink of water, Jesus likened himself to the source that was able to quench mankind's real thirst:

'If you only knew what God is offering
and who it is that is saying to you:
"Give me a drink",
you would have been the one to ask,
and he would have given you living water'.

When the woman replied, showing that she was still thinking of the water that was in Jacob's well, Jesus continued:

'Whoever drinks this water
will get thirsty again;
but anyone who drinks the water that I shall give
will never be thirsty again:
the water that I shall give
will turn into a spring within him, welling up to
eternal life'. (John 4.10, 13–14)

The concept of our Lord Jesus Christ as the source from whom flows out the life of the Spirit, bringing joy to all mankind and health to the whole universe, finds classic expression in the vision of John recorded in the twenty-second chapter of the book of Revelation. This vision had been foreshadowed when Ezekiel, living in exile in Babylon, foresaw the restoration of the Jerusalem Temple, with the water of life flowing out from under the right side of the altar. This copious stream gave fertility to the land on the banks of the river and provided life and habitat for a multitude of fish.

When we contemplate our Lord's descent into the waters of the Jordan, our imagination finds ready to hand a whole wealth of biblical imagery to help us penetrate the meaning of the mystery.

But we face a problem that has often perplexed Christians down the centuries. All of the biblical images we have cited tell of life, of imparting the life of the Spirit. Our Lord Jesus had no need to have this life imparted to him, for he was himself the source of that life. Besides this, in Holy Scripture water has another significance: it is a sign and means of cleansing, of purifying from sin. For example, the prophet Ezekiel in another passage writes: 'I shall pour clean water over you and you will be cleansed; I shall cleanse you of all your defilement and all your idols. I shall give you a new heart, and put a new spirit in you' (Ezekiel 36.25–6); and, in the story of the Flood, water is not so much a purifying agent as a destroyer. The great waters of the Flood did not cleanse the wicked people on the earth but drowned them. When our Lord descended into the waters of the Jordan, was he submitting to purification or judgement? He certainly was not, for he was sinless and, more than that, he was the source of the new life of the Spirit which Ezekiel had prophesied would one day be poured out upon mankind. These facts pose us a problem which we must try to solve.

St John the Baptist was the first to express the perplexity we have just described. When Jesus presented himself for baptism John said, 'It is I who need baptism from you, and yet you come to me!' Jesus replied, 'Leave it like this for the time being; it is fitting that we should, in this way, do all that righteousness demands'.

We should 'do all that righteousness demands'. Jesus was not seeking through John's baptism to acquire righteousness for himself; he submitted to John's baptism in order to demonstrate how men and women would be able to acquire righteousness. The first thing that was necessary was that he, the incarnate Word of God, identify himself with the human race.

By joining the crowd of sinners who were thronging to be baptized in the Jordan he declared his solidarity with the human race, and proclaimed his readiness to take upon himself all the consequences of sin. His joining the crowd on the banks of the river Jordan was the sign of his being 'made sin for us'. Doing this, however, he did not in the slightest degree lose his sinlessness. It was only because he was and remained sinless that his identification with us brought about the destruction of sin in us.

Having identified himself in this way with the human race, he then showed how men and women can become joined with his righteousness through his having become united with our humanity, and in particular by his having offered that humanity in sacrifice on the cross, a sacrifice which was rewarded by this human nature being raised up into everlasting life. Our Lord's going down into the water signified his death, and his coming up out of the water signified his Resurrection.

His baptism therefore was a foreshadowing both of the paschal mystery and of the Christian sacrament of baptism, in which the Christian goes down with Christ into his death and rises with him to new life. 'When we were baptised in Christ Jesus we were baptised in his death; in other words, when we were baptised we went into the tomb with him and joined him in death, so that as Christ was raised from the dead by the Father's glory, we too might live a new life' (Romans 6.3–4). In baptism the Christian is mystically united with Christ, but such union is possible only because the sinless, eternal Word of God became united with human nature at that moment when Jesus was conceived in the womb of the virgin Mary. It is this union of the eternal Word of God with human nature that Jesus expressed by his readiness to join the crowd who came to be baptized by John in the Jordan. He then, in the actual baptism, added to this demonstration of solidarity with us an action–sermon which symbolically represented his death and Resurrection, and foreshadowed the sacrament which would make his death and Resurrection effective for believers.

There is another element in this foreshadowing of the paschal mystery: the descent of the Holy Spirit. The baptism scene at the Jordan points not only to our Lord's passion, death and Resurrection, but also to the descent of the Holy Spirit upon the Church, for the paschal mystery was not complete until the fruit of the acts on the cross was manifested in the birth of the new people of God.

At his baptism in the Jordan the Holy Spirit descended upon Jesus, we are told, 'in bodily form'. The phrase 'in bodily form' is significant. As the Word of God, the eternal Son of the Father, our Lord is for ever in union with the Father in the bond of love that is the Holy Spirit. In one sense, therefore, he had no need to receive the Holy Spirit, but in another sense, because he 'emptied himself to assume the condition of a slave, and became as men are' (Philippians 2.7), in his human nature he required the strength of the Holy Spirit to enable him to fulfil his destiny. Seeking the help of the Holy Spirit was a sign of his humility. And besides this, he could only hand on the Holy Spirit to men and women through his flesh. In receiving the Holy Spirit 'in bodily form' he was receiving that Spirit on our behalf and not on account of any defect in himself, just as he, perfectly sinless, had taken our guilt upon himself when he received baptism. Our Lord's reception of the Holy Spirit 'in bodily form' corresponds to his conferring the Spirit upon the Church through his body when, having died on the cross, he gave birth to the Church in the blood and water that flowed from his pierced side.

The grand action–sermon preached by the baptism of Jesus in the Jordan proclaims how every human soul and indeed the human race can be restored through Christian baptism to the state of righteousness in which it was created in the beginning.

Our Lord's baptism in the Jordan possesses also a cosmic dimension. He let himself be immersed in water, the element that is life itself. The Word, through whom all that is was created, descended into that which to our minds is the most elemental of all things, and imparted to it the virtue of eternal life. By touching the waters of the Jordan he imparted new life to the universe.

The descent of the Word into his own creation is symbolized during the Easter Vigil when, at the rite of baptism, the paschal candle is lowered three times into the water of the font. In his letter to the Roman Christians St Paul writes a moving comment on the concept of cosmic recreation through Christ. We associate the thought of rebirth in Christ usually with the rebirth of individuals, but St Paul gives rebirth through baptism a wider meaning.

> The whole creation is eagerly waiting for God to reveal his sons. It was not for any fault on the part of creation that it was made unable to attain its purpose, it was made so by God; but creation still retains the hope of being freed, like us, from its slavery to decadence, to enjoy the same freedom and glory as the children of God. From the beginning till now the entire creation, as we know, has been groaning in one great act of giving birth.
>
> (Romans 8.19–22)

JESUS IS BAPTISED IN THE RIVER JORDAN: MATTHEW 3.13–17

Then Jesus appeared: he came from Galilee to the Jordan to be baptised by John. John tried to dissuade him. 'It is I who need baptism from you' he said 'and you come to me!' But Jesus replied, 'Leave it like this for the time being; it is fitting that we should, in this way, do all that righteousness demands'. At this, John gave in to him.

As soon as Jesus was baptised he came up from the water, and suddenly the heavens opened and he saw the Spirit of God descending like a dove and coming down on him. And a voice spoke from heaven, 'This is my Son, the Beloved; my favour rests on him'.

2

The Wedding at Cana

The primeval wedding: Genesis 2.18–24
Yahweh God said, 'It is not good that the man should be alone. I will make him a helpmate.' So from the soil Yahweh God fashioned all the wild beasts and all the birds of heaven. These he brought to the man to see what he would call them; each one was to bear the name the man would give it. The man gave names to all the cattle, all the birds of heaven and all the wild beasts. But no helpmate suitable for man was found for him. So Yahweh God made the man fall into a deep sleep. And while he slept, he took one of his ribs and enclosed it in flesh. Yahweh God built the rib he had taken from the man into a woman, and brought her to the man. The man exclaimed:

'This at last is bone from my bones,
and flesh from my flesh!
This is to be called woman,
for this was taken from man.'

This is why a man leaves his father and mother and joins himself to his wife, and they become one body.

The Hour of Jesus: John 17.1–5
After saying this, Jesus raised his eyes to heaven and said:

'Father, the hour has come:
glorify your Son
so that your Son may glorify you;
and, through the power over all mankind that you
    have given him,
let him give eternal life to all those you have
    entrusted to him.
And eternal life is this:
to know you,
the only true God,
and Jesus Christ whom you have sent.
I have glorified you on earth
and finished the work
that you gave me to do.
Now, Father, it is time for you to glorify me
with that glory I had with you
before ever the world was.'

The Messianic banquet: Isaiah 25.6–8a
On this mountain,
Yahweh Sabaoth will prepare for all peoples
a banquet of rich food, a banquet of fine wines,
of food rich and juicy, of fine strained wines.
On this mountain he will remove
the mourning veil covering all peoples,
and the shroud enwrapping all nations,
he will destroy Death for ever.

The bride of Yahweh: Isaiah 62.3–5
You are to be a crown of splendour in the hand of
    Yahweh,
a princely diadem in the hand of your God;
no longer are you to be named 'Forsaken',
nor your land 'Abandoned',
but you shall be called 'My Delight'

and your land 'The Wedded';
for Yahweh takes delight in you
and your land will have its wedding.

Like a young man marrying a virgin,
so will the one who built you wed you,
and as the bridegroom rejoices in his bride,
so will your God rejoice in you.

Wine is life for man: Ecclesiasticus 31.25–9
  Do not play the valiant at your wine,
    for wine has been the undoing of many.
  The furnace proves the temper of steel,
    and wine proves hearts in the drinking bouts of
      braggarts.
  Wine is life for man
    if drunk in moderation.
  What is life worth without wine?
    It was created to make men happy.
  Drunk at the right time and in the right amount,
    wine makes for a glad heart and a cheerful mind.
  Bitterness of soul comes of wine drunk to excess
    out of temper or bravado.

MEDITATION

The happenings at the wedding feast at Cana in Galilee are associated in the devotional imagination of the Church with the feast of the Epiphany and of the Baptism of our Lord, for what happened at Cana was an epiphany: 'He let his glory be seen, and his disciples believed in him' (John 2.11).

In his Gospel St John places the incident at Cana at the end of the first week of our Lord's appearance in public. St John gives us a day-by-day account of that week. Although it is not stated explicitly, it would seem that Jesus had very recently been baptized by John, perhaps at the beginning of the week or very shortly before it began. On the first day of the week John is found facing interrogation by the delegation from Jerusalem, asking if he is the Christ and, if not, by what authority he is baptizing. He speaks about one who is coming, who is in fact already among them, one who is much greater than he is. On the second day of that week John declares that this one who will follow him is the lamb of God who will take away the sin of the world and who will baptize with the Holy Spirit. On the third day John points out Jesus, the lamb of God, to two of his own disciples, who then leave him and follow Jesus. It would appear that as soon as he had baptized Jesus, John was moved to proclaim that Jesus was the Christ. In this way, John, the last of the great prophets of the old dispensation, made our Lord's glory to be seen.

On the fourth day the circle of those who are turning towards Jesus widens and on that day, St John tells us, Jesus decided to go north to Galilee, his home province. No doubt he had been reminded of the wedding that was about to take place and which he was expected to attend. Jesus set off in haste, for Cana was some distance from the place where John was baptizing, and three days later he arrived in Cana to attend the wedding.

At the wedding Mary, the mother of Jesus, was present. Jesus and his mother were probably relatives of the bride or groom. When Mary gave directions to the servants they appear to have accepted her authority, as though they knew her; and when the wine ran out she immediately shared the embarrassment that the family must have felt. She turned to her Son and asked him to do something about it.

Her Son's reply has been translated in various ways. The *Revised Standard Version* has 'O woman, what have you to do with me?' the *New Revised Standard Version* has 'Woman, what concern is that to you and to me?' and the *Jerusalem Bible* has 'Woman, why turn to me?' Older translations gave the impression that Jesus was almost snubbing his mother. The more recent translations have got rid of that overtone. There was nothing in the least brusque in our Lord's reply. In his commentary on John's Gospel James McPolin SJ explains that, taking into account Old Testament parallels, a good translation would be 'What is the relationship between you and me', a rhetorical question that invites speculation. Jesus may well have been hinting at the unique relationship that was to exist between himself and his mother. McPolin adds: 'The reply of Jesus to his mother is not discourteous or harsh; neither is it a refusal, because she did not ask anything of him; nor is it a reproach, because Jesus takes the initiative and works a miracle'.

The second part of our Lord's reply to his mother was: 'My hour has not yet come.' The hour of Jesus was the 'hour' of his passion, death and resurrection. St John reports that Jesus attended this wedding 'Three days later', an allusion to the three days the disciples waited for his rising from the dead, the hour when his glory was clearly seen. The miracle at Cana should be seen, therefore, not as the coming of his hour, but as a foreshadowing of that hour. In this miracle he gave the disciples a glimpse of his glory, and thereby set their faith alight.

The miracle underlines the truth that John the Baptist had already preached: the utter superiority of the baptism of Jesus over the baptism that John was able to give. The baptism of repentance administered by John compared to baptism in the Spirit which Jesus was to institute was as water is to wine. In general, the entire system of ritual purification practised by the Jews, and symbolized by the six water pots at the wedding feast, was to be superseded by the sacramental system of the Christian Faith. The miracle of changing the water into wine is like a commentary on the text in the Letter to the Hebrews:

> The blood of goats and bulls and the ashes of a heifer are sprinkled on those who have incurred defilement and they restore the holiness of their outward lives; how much more effectively the blood of Christ, who offered himself as the perfect sacrifice to God through the eternal Spirit, can purify our inner selves from dead actions so that we do our service to the living God.
>
> (Hebrews 9.13–14)

In this miracle there may also be an allusion to the wine of the Eucharist, which will become the blood of the new covenant.

The prominence of wine in this episode of the gospel story is an indication also that our Lord is proclaiming the advent of the Messianic age. In the Old Testament wine is described as that which makes men cheerful (Psalm 104.15). Mankind will know true gladness when the Messiah comes. Many passages in the Old Testament describe the Messianic age as a time when great prosperity will be known, the earth will be fertile and productive, and wine will flow in abundance. Examples of Old Testament visions of the Messianic age are given above. Speaking of the inauguration of the Messianic age the prophet Joel declares:

> When that day comes
> the mountains will run with new wine.

The Messianic age is likened also to a marriage, and the Lord himself is seen as the husband of his people:

> For now your creator will be your husband,
> his name, Yahweh Sabaoth;
> your redeemer will be the Holy One of Israel,
> he is called the God of the whole earth.
> Yes, like a forsaken wife, distressed in spirit,
> Yahweh calls you back.
> Does a man cast off the wife of his youth?
> says your God. (Isaiah 54.5–6)

So much for the meaning of the miracle of the changing water into wine at a wedding feast. The incident tells us also about the place of Mary, the mother of Jesus, in God's plan for the salvation of mankind. The fact that Jesus addresses Mary as 'Woman' and that the narrator refers to her as 'the mother of Jesus' is significant. 'Woman' was a title full of meaning for those steeped in biblical tradition. 'The woman' in Genesis 3.15 against whom and against whose offspring the devil's hatred was aroused is the woman whom Adam named Eve, a name derived from the Hebrew verb meaning 'to live'. She was the mother of all the living. In the episode we are considering, Mary is introduced not by her name, but as 'the mother of Jesus'. Such a way of speaking about a woman focused on her son, and this manner of speech, James McPolin SJ tells us, was 'a complimentary title for a woman who has been fortunate enough to bear a son'.

One might think that because St John mentions Mary only twice in the course of his Gospel, that he considered her unimportant. The contrary is the truth, because by limiting reference to her in this way, St John portrays her as the framework within which the work of her Son is carried out. On his first public appearance she quietly intercedes with him to save the host of the feast embarrassment and to restore joy to the disappointed wedding guests, while at the same time announcing, symbolically, the advent of the Messianic age and giving those present a glimpse of his glory. She appears again only at the consummation of his work of redemption, when again, as she stands at the foot of the cross, St John refers to her as 'the mother of Jesus'. Once again Jesus addresses her as 'Woman'. 'Woman, this is your son' Jesus says to her and to John, 'This is your mother'. She has become the new Eve, now mother of all who live in the Spirit, and her motherly intercession still paves the way for the redemptive work of her Son.

IT HAD TURNED INTO WINE:
JOHN 2.1–11

*Three days later there was a wedding at Cana
in Galilee. The mother of Jesus was there, and
Jesus and his disciples had also been invited.
When they ran out of wine, since the wine
provided for the wedding was all finished, the
mother of Jesus said to him, 'They have no
wine'. Jesus said, ' Woman, why turn to me?
My hour has not come yet.' His mother said to
the servants, 'Do whatever he tells you'. There
were six stone water jars standing there, meant
for the ablutions that are customary among the
Jews: each could hold twenty or thirty gallons.
Jesus said to the servants, 'Fill the jars with
water', and they filled them to the brim. 'Draw
some out now' he told them ' and take it to the
steward.' They did this; the steward tasted the
water, and it had turned into wine. Having no
idea where it came from — only the servants
who had drawn the water knew — the steward
called the bridegroom and said, 'People gener-
ally serve the best wine first, and keep the
cheaper sort till the guests have had plenty to*

*drink; but you have kept the best wine till now'.
This was the first of the signs given by Jesus: it
was given at Cana in Galilee. He let his glory
be seen, and his disciples believed in him.*

3

The Proclamation of the Kingdom of God

The kingdom of David: 2 Samuel 7.8–16

'This is what you must say to my servant David, "Yahweh Sabaoth says this: I took you from the pasture, from following the sheep, to be leader of my people Israel; I have been with you on all your expeditions; I have cut off all your enemies before you. I will give you fame as great as the fame of the greatest on earth. I will provide a place for my people Israel; I will plant them there and they shall dwell in that place and never be disturbed again; nor shall the wicked continue to oppress them as they did, in the days when I appointed judges over my people Israel; I will give them rest from all their enemies. Yahweh will make you great; Yahweh will make you a House. And when your days are ended and you are laid to rest with your ancestors, I will preserve the offspring of your body after you and make his sovereignty secure. (It is he who shall build a house for my name, and I will make his royal throne secure for ever.) I will be a father to him and he a son to me; if he does evil, I will punish him with the rod such as men use, with strokes such as mankind gives. Yet I will not withdraw my favour from him, as I withdrew it from your predecessor. Your House and your sovereignty will always stand secure before me and your throne be established for ever." '

A covenant with David: Psalm 89.20–9
> 'I have selected my servant David
> and anointed him with my holy oil;
> my hand will be constantly with him,
> he will be able to rely on my arm.
>
> 'No enemy will be able to outwit him,
> no wicked man to worst him,
> I myself will crush his opponents,
> I will strike dead all who hate him.
>
> 'With my faithfulness and love,
> his fortunes shall rise in my name.
> I will give him control of the sea,
> complete control of the rivers.
>
> 'He will invoke me, "My father,
> my God and rock of my safety",
> and I shall make him my first-born,
> the Most High for kings on earth.'

The Son of Man: Daniel 7.13–14
> 'I gazed into the visions of the night.
> And I saw, coming on the clouds of heaven,
> one like a son of man.
> He came to the one of great age
> and was led into his presence.
> On him was conferred sovereignty,
> glory and kingship,
> and men of all peoples, nations and languages
>   became his servants.
> His sovereignty is an eternal sovereignty
> which shall never pass away,
> nor will his empire ever be destroyed.'

'Hold your heads high': Luke 21.25-8
'There will be signs in the sun and moon and stars; on earth nations in agony, bewildered by the clamour of the ocean and its waves; men dying of fear as they await what

menaces the world, for the powers of heaven will be shaken. And then they will see the Son of Man coming in a cloud with power and great glory. When these things begin to take place, stand erect, hold your heads high, because your liberation is near at hand.'

The keys of the kingdom: Matthew 16.13–20
When Jesus came to the region of Caesarea Philippi he put this question to his disciples, 'Who do people say the Son of Man is?' And they said, 'Some say he is John the Baptist, some Elijah, and others Jeremiah or one of the prophets'. 'But you,' he said, 'who do you say I am?' The Simon Peter spoke up, 'You are the Christ,' he said 'the Son of the living God'. Jesus replied, 'Simon son of Jonah, you are a happy man! Because it was not flesh and blood that revealed this to you but my Father in heaven. So I now say to you: You are Peter and on this rock I will build my Church. And the gates of the underworld can never hold out against it. I will give you the keys of the kingdom of heaven: whatever you bind on earth shall be considered bound in heaven; whatever you loose on earth shall be considered loosed in heaven.' Then he gave the disciples strict orders not to tell anyone that he was the Christ.

MEDITATION

Most of the Mysteries of the Rosary present an incident that takes place within a well-defined geographical setting. When meditating upon these mysteries it is easy to apply the method of St Ignatius, and begin by fixing the imagination upon the scene. This is what Ignatius calls 'composition of place'. Meditation moves on beyond this stage, it is true, but that is normally a very good way to approach meditation. To attach a physical image to the third Mystery of Light is not easy. The Gospels report that our Lord's proclamation of the kingdom of God was the prologue to his preaching in Galilee, to which province he had returned soon after his temptations in the wilderness of Judaea, and after he heard that John the Baptist had been arrested. In this mystery we are invited to focus our mind upon the meaning of the word used by our Lord rather than upon place and action.

The words he spoke as he inaugurated his preaching of the kingdom are almost the same in Matthew and in Mark. 'Repent, for the kingdom of heaven is close at hand' (Matthew 4.17); 'The time has come and the kingdom of God is close at hand. Repent, and believe the Good News' (Mark 1.15). There is a double statement here: first, that the kingdom of God is about to break in upon mankind, and second, that its coming challenges all men and women to repent. Meditation upon our Lord's proclamation of the kingdom of God must therefore include a consideration of what he meant by 'repent' and what he meant by 'kingdom'.

Our Lord's call to repentance is where his message over-laps that of John the Baptist's; and on the first occasion when Jesus sent the Twelve out to preach he sent them not to announce that his kingdom had come, but simply to preach repentance. 'So they set off to preach repentance' (Mark 6.12). The Good News could not be fully announced until after the resurrection of Jesus from the dead. That is why, in his initial proclamation of the kingdom, according to both Matthew and Mark Jesus said, 'The kingdom of God is *close at hand*.'

Although membership in the kingdom that our Lord was about to inaugurate would allow men and women to share in the life of his Holy Spirit, a benefit that John's baptism of repentance could never have bestowed, the repentance which John demanded for the efficacy of his baptism was the same repentance as would be demanded from those who would seek membership in the kingdom of God through Christian baptism. In calling men and women to repentance John the Baptist and then Jesus were following a spiritual tradition that reached back into primeval times. From the earliest times men and women knew that they had sinned against God and were called upon to feel shame and to seek forgiveness; and every spiritual leader ever sent to help men and women on their way to salvation based his message upon a call to repentance. In Israel the preaching of the prophets was a continuous invitation to repentance. Our Lord's proclamation of his kingdom followed in unbroken continu-ity from this ancient tradition. Repentance was thus the springboard from which the Good News of Christ's kingdom had to be launched.

A Greek New Testament dictionary defines the Greek word used for repentance in this way; 'a change of mind' or 'a change in the inner man'. Repentance is more than simply an admission of fault and a request for forgiveness; it must include the desire to turn away from sin and from all the attachments that lead one to sin. In effect it is the first impulse towards ceasing to live for oneself and beginning to live for love of God and of others.

Luke's account of our Lord's first preaching does not contain a proclamation of the kingdom in the same words as those used by Matthew and Mark; none the less his first public declaration as reported by Luke amounted to a proclamation of the coming of the kingdom of God; and it is Luke who supplies action and a physical setting in which to place this proclamation. On a sabbath day in the synagogue at his home town of Nazareth, Jesus read from the prophet Isaiah and applied the text to himself. He claimed to be the anointed of God, who had come at last to

> proclaim liberty to captives
> and to the blind new sight,
> to set the downtrodden free,
> to proclaim the Lord's year of favour. (Luke 4.18)

This was the manner in which he announced that he was bringing the kingdom of God into the world. If we find it helpful in meditating on this mystery to begin by focusing on a physical scene, we can use this passage in Luke 4.16–30. St Luke's account provides not only a physical setting for our Lord's words, but recounts action and dialogue, all of which stimulate meditation.

Our Lord's words as recorded in Luke's Gospel at first won approval. The people were filled with pride at the thought of one of their own boys becoming the Messiah; but when he began to contrast his own race unfavourably with pagans, citing examples from the Old Testament, many turned against him and attempted to kill him. The prophecy of Simeon, that the child Jesus was 'destined to be a sign that is rejected' (Luke 2.34), was already being fulfilled in the very moment when Jesus announced in the synagogue of his home town that he had come to fulfil the promises concerning the coming of the kingdom. In the very act of proclaiming the advent of his kingdom, our Lord provoked the enmity of the kingdom of darkness.

From this incident at Nazareth we learn that membership of the kingdom of God does not mean being enlisted in the winning side so that we may enjoy privileges, as the congregation in the Nazareth synagogue had at first thought, but means being enlisted in the army of the Prince of Light, which will be engaged in battle against the forces of the Prince of Darkness for as long as this world lasts. This enlistment brings not privilege but pain.

We now consider the word 'kingdom'. The 'kingdom of God' and ' the kingdom of heaven' have exactly the same meaning. Out of reverence, the Jews hesitated to use the name of God, and so they replaced that name with 'heaven'. That same sensitivity is echoed in the New Testament.

The notion of kingdom and of kingship has its roots in the Old Testament. After they had gained possession of the Promised Land, where at first they established a tribal confederacy, the Israelites were proud of the fact that that they had no earthly king; their king was Yahweh, the God who was above all the gods of the pagans. As time went on and they found that they could not effectively oppose the power of other races, of the Philistines in particular, they demanded that they be given a king who could unite the tribes of the confederacy and co-ordinate their efforts in battle. At first the prophet Samuel opposed this demand; the people persisted, and Samuel reluctantly acceded to their request, but warned them of the dangers they would face, for no earthly king would be a perfect vice-regent for Yahweh, and no earthly kingdom, even under the most perfect of kings, would perfectly manifest the kingdom of God. The subsequent history of Israel, the people of God, is the story of a people who, under rulers of varying degrees of virtue, tried to form and maintain upon earth a society that was faithful to the covenant.

The record of the history of Israel as we find it in the Old Testament can best be described as a philosophy of history, the underlying thesis of which was that when the people were faithful to the covenant with Yahweh, they prospered: when they were disobedient, they suffered under foreign oppressors.

In spite of the warning and scepticism of the prophet Samuel, Scripture states plainly that God was with his people and their rulers. Yahweh promised them his support. The classic example of this is Yahweh's promise, through the prophet Nathan, to King David. This is recorded in the second book of Samuel, and is celebrated also in Psalm 89. Although there is insistence on the faithfulness to the law of God of the heirs to the Davidic throne, even if any of them should become faithless the promise to his dynasty will not be withdrawn.

The ultimate confirmation of the firmness of God's promise to David came when the angel Gabriel declared that Mary's child would sit upon the throne of David and that his kingdom would have no end; but before this final flowering of the kingship of David was to be achieved, the concept of the kingdom of God went through several stages of refinement in the later Old Testament period, and there is much to learn from that development.

At an early stage the Israelites were forced to reflect on the meaning of kingdom and kingship through the chastening experience of schism. After David's death the kingdom split in two. From that time until the conquest of Samaria by the Assyrians in 721 BC there were two kingdoms : Israel in the north and Judah in the south. On the whole the southern kingdom kept faith with Yahweh better than the northern kingdom, but eventually its sins brought God's wrath down upon it too and Jerusalem fell to the Neo-Babylonians in 587 BC. By 581 BC most of the people had been deported to Babylonia and the great exile began. From this time onwards there developed a spiritualizing of the concept of the kingdom of God. This process had already begun under the influence of the great eighth and seventh-century prophets, but it gathered strength in the time of exile when devout people, the 'remnant', were forced to reflect on the meaning of their faith. A great figure of this era was the prophet Ezekiel.

With the return from exile and the rebuilding of the Temple towards the end of the sixth century BC, a Jewish state was formed, but it was a state under Persian sovereignty and its ethos was different from what it had been in former ages. There was a secular governor and also a High Priest. In effect the state was a religious community ruled over by the High Priest and the ecclesiastical authorities, and although the Temple rituals were reinstated, the status of synagogue worship, centred on the reading of the Scriptures, was enhanced. During the exile this was the only form of worship that had been available to the people, and it was in that period also that much work had been done in collecting and editing the Old Testament as we now know it. The kingdom of Yahweh began to be regarded more as the community of those who were faithful to his law than as a political state.

From this time onwards the eyes of the devout, of the 'remnant', the 'poor', those who 'looked forward to Israel's comforting' (Luke 2.15), began to seek the kingdom of God not in this world but beyond it. There were still many fanatical nationalists, it is true, who hoped for the establishment of a Jewish state that would dominate all others, and it was from people who thought like this that Jesus escaped back to the hills and hid himself when they wanted to make him king, having seen the miracle of the feeding of the multitude (John 6.14–15); but the eschatological dimension of the concept of the kingdom of God had gripped the imagination of the truly devout in Israel.

The urge to look beyond this world for the perfect kingdom of God was encouraged greatly by the terrible persecution the Jews suffered under the Seleucid kings, and it is to that period that visions of the Son of Man which are recorded in the book of Daniel belong. The visions recorded in this book describe how all of the kingdoms of this world will destroy and succeed one another until all have passed away. The Son of Man is truly man, but he comes on clouds of glory, he is also from God, he is God; and his kingdom is not of this world. Our Lord Jesus stated this explicitly; 'Mine is not a kingdom of this world' (John 18.36). Jesus is indeed the fulfilment of this late Jewish vision of the Son of Man, who is also the Messiah and the Suffering Servant of Yahweh.

At the end of a long life, St John the Evangelist had visions of the kingdom of God which continue and perfect the visionary tradition of late Judaism. Heaven and earth are re-created, and the future of the world is entrusted to the Lamb who is the King of kings, and whose praise is sung in these words:

> 'You are worthy to take the scroll
> and break the seals of it,
> because you were sacrificed, and with your blood
> you bought men for God
> of every race, language, people and nation
> and made them a line of kings and priests,
> to serve our God and to rule the world'.
>
> (Revelation 5.9)

We learn from the Scriptures that the kingdom of God in its fullness can come to be only at the end when all things will have been made new; and yet the Scriptures also insist that this kingdom or rule of God is now perfectly at work in this world and in the hearts of individuals. The world and all men and women have been handed over to the rule of Jesus Christ, the Son of the eternal Father.

That rule is exercised pre-eminently through his body on earth, that is, through his Church. Most significant in the hymn in praise of the Lamb are these words: 'made them a line of kings and priests, to serve God and to rule the world'. Kingship and priesthood are linked: ruling has become equated with serving. 'If I, then, the Lord and Master, have washed your feet, you should wash each other's feet. I have given you an example so that you may copy what I have done to you' (John 13.14–15).

So often in the past Christians have thought that the rule of Christ on earth is to be accomplished by the establish-ment of a theocratic state that claims to be Christian. As citi-zens Christians must seek to create states that are governed according to the law of God, but to think that the perfect kingdom of God can be established politically is an illusion. The perfection of God's rule upon earth is effected through the word and sacraments of the Church, and the true kingdom of God is built up in as much as the faithful diligently live by the power of the word and the sacraments. Our best guides to understanding how the Church is the realization of the kingdom in time are the parables of the kingdom as we find these in Matthew chapter 6. These parables are also parables of the Church, because the Church is the kingdom of God in embryo, and so, because its life is the life of the Holy Spirit, it is perfect: yet while still maturing on earth it has to endure the presence amongst its members of noxious weeds, and, even within individual members who are destined for sanctity, purification is always in progress. The kingdom of God is not of this world, but it is in the world. Were it not so the world would have no hope.

THE KINGDOM OF HEAVEN:
MATTHEW 13.24–30

He put another parable before them, 'The kingdom of heaven may be compared to a man who sowed good seed in his field. While everybody was asleep his enemy came, sowed darnel all among the wheat, and made off. When the new wheat sprouted and ripened, the darnel appeared as well. The owner's servants went to him and said, "Sir, was it not good seed that you sowed in your field? If so, where does the darnel come from?" "Some enemy has done this" he answered. And the servants said, "Do you want us to go and weed it out?" But he said, "No, because when you weed out the darnel you might pull up the wheat with it. Let them both grow till the harvest; and at harvest time I shall say to the reapers: First collect the darnel and tie it in bundles to be burnt, then gather the wheat into my barn."'

4

The Transfiguration

Moses ascends Sinai: Exodus 24.12–18
Yahweh said to Moses, 'Come up to me on the mountain and stay there while I give you the stone tablets – the law and the commandments – that I have written for their instruction'. Accordingly Moses rose, he and his servant Joshua, and they went up the mountain of God. To the elders he had said, 'Wait here for us until we come back to you. You have Aaron and Hur with you; if anyone has a difference to settle, let him go to them.' And Moses went up the mountain.

The cloud covered the mountain, and the glory of Yahweh settled on the mountain of Sinai; for six days the cloud covered it, and on the seventh day Yahweh called to Moses from inside the cloud. To the eyes of the sons of Israel the glory of Yahweh seemed like a devouring fire on the mountain top. Moses went right into the cloud. He went up the mountain, and stayed there for forty days and forty nights.

Moses returns from the mountain: Exodus 34.29–35
When Moses came down from the mountain of Sinai – as he came down from the mountain, Moses had the two tablets of the Testimony in his hands – he did not know that the skin on his face was radiant after speaking with Yahweh. And when Aaron and all the sons of Israel saw Moses, the skin on his face shone so much that they

would not venture near him. But Moses called to them, and Aaron with all the leaders of the community came back to him; and he spoke to them. Then all the sons of Israel came closer, and he passed on to them all the orders that Yahweh had given him on the mountain of Sinai. And when Moses had finished speaking to them, he put a veil over his face. Whenever he went into Yahweh's presence to speak with him, Moses would remove the veil until he came out again. And when he came out, he would tell the sons of Israel what he had been ordered to pass on to them, and the sons of Israel would see the face of Moses radiant. Then Moses would put the veil back over his face until he returned to speak with Yahweh.

The mountain of the Messiah: Isaiah 11.1–9
    A shoot springs from the stock of Jesse,
a scion thrusts from his roots:
on him the spirit of Yahweh rests,
a spirit of wisdom and insight,
a spirit of counsel and power,
a spirit of knowledge and of the fear of Yahweh.
(The fear of Yahweh is his breath.)
He does not judge by appearances,
he gives no verdict on hearsay,
but judges the wretched with integrity,
and with equity gives a verdict for the poor
    of the land.
His word is a rod that strikes the ruthless,
his sentences bring death to the wicked.

Integrity is the loincloth round his waist,
faithfulness the belt about his hips.

The wolf lives with the lamb,
the panther lies down with the kid,
calf and lion cub feed together
with a little boy to lead them.
The cow and the bear make friends,

their young lie down together.
The lion eats straw like the ox.
The infant plays over the cobra's hole;
into the viper's lair
the young child puts his hand.
They do no hurt, no harm,
on all my holy mountain,
for the country is filled with the knowledge of
    Yahweh
as the waters swell the sea.

Eye-witnesses: 2 Peter 1.16–18
It was not any cleverly invented myths that we were
repeating when we brought you the knowledge of the
power and the coming of our Lord Jesus Christ; we had
seen his majesty for ourselves. He was honoured and
glorified by God the Father, when the Sublime Glory itself
spoke to him and said, 'This is my Son, the Beloved; he
enjoys my favour'. We heard this ourselves, spoken from
heaven, when we were with him on the holy mountain.

Jesus teaches: the people listen: Matthew 5.1–12
Seeing the crowds, he went up the hill. There he sat down
and was joined by his disciples. Then he began to speak.
This is what he taught them:

'How happy are the poor in spirit;
theirs is the kingdom of heaven.
Happy the gentle:
they shall have the earth for their heritage.
Happy those who mourn:
they shall be comforted.
Happy those who hunger and thirst for what is right:
they shall be satisfied.
Happy the merciful:
they shall have mercy shown them.
Happy the pure in heart:
they shall see God.

Happy the peacemakers:
they shall be called sons of God.
Happy those who are persecuted in the cause of
   right:
theirs is the kingdom of heaven.

'Happy are you when people abuse you and persecute you and speak all kinds of calumny against you on my account. Rejoice and be glad, for your reward will be great in heaven; this is how they persecuted the prophets before you.'

MEDITATION

The fourth Mystery of Light in contrast to the third is placed against a very distinct physical background. The scene is set upon a mountain, and the action begins with the ascent of the mountain by Jesus and three disciples, Peter and James and John, the three whom he again called apart from the rest, to be with him during his agony in the garden of Gethsemane. The presence with him of these three points to the importance of the occasion. The transfiguration episode is indeed one of the most important events recorded in the Gospels. This is acknowledged by the inclusion in the Lectionary for the Roman Missal of the relevant Gospel reading on the second Sunday in Lent on each year of the three-year cycle, and by the annual commemoration of the Transfiguration on 6 August.

The image of the mountain is itself evocative. There are few people who do not feel elated when they lift their eyes up to view a mountain range, and few who do not at some time in their lives feel an urge to climb a mountain. The word 'mountain' occurs very often in the pages of the Bible.

> Who has the right to climb the mountain of Yahweh,
> who the right to stand in his holy place?
> He whose hands are clean, whose heart is pure,
> whose soul does not pay homage to worthless things
> and who never swears to a lie. (Psalm 24.3–4)

Climbing up a mountain is a symbol of growing in virtue and

coming ever closer to God. The centre for worship for the Israelites was the hill of Zion. Yahweh Sabaoth, we are told, 'dwells on Mount Zion' (Isaiah 8.18); and the Old Testament speaks of the tribes of God 'going up' to Jerusalem to offer prayer and sacrifice. But it is not just Israelites who go up to worship the one, true God:

In the days to come
the mountain of the Temple of Yahweh
shall tower above the mountains
and be lifted higher than the hills.
All the nations will stream to it,
peoples without number will come to it; and they will
    say:
'Come, let us go up to the mountain of Yahweh,
to the Temple of the God of Jacob
that he may teach us his ways
so that we may walk in his paths;
since the Law will go out from Zion,
and the oracle of Yahweh from Jerusalem'.
                                        (Isaiah 2.2–3)

St Matthew reports our Lord's first miracle of the multiplication of loaves and then tells us that, 'After sending the crowds away he went up into the hills by himself to pray' (Matthew 14.23). Jesus himself was brought up to appreciate the tradition of his people, and knew the suitability of the mountain, or even a hill, as a place in which to pray and be in the presence of his Father in heaven.

The incident upon which we now meditate marks a turning-point in our Lord's programme. For some time he had been preaching the advent of his kingdom in Galilee; now the time was approaching when, although preaching and teaching would still have a place, it was action that would become vital. He was about to set his face resolutely to go up to Jerusalem, the city of sacrifice; and it was to prepare the apostles for this most momentous phase in their lives that Jesus made a little detour and led Peter and James and John away to be by themselves on a mountain-top where they could pray. In the hour of desolation when they had laid the body of Jesus in the tomb on the first Good Friday, their memory of the extraordinary vision on the mount of transfiguration may be what saved them from utter collapse. This view is expressed by Pope St Leo the Great in one of his sermons. 'By changing his appearance in this way he chiefly wished to prevent his disciples from feeling scandalized in their hearts by the cross. He did not want the disgrace of the passion, which he freely accepted, to break their faith. This is why he revealed to them the excellence of his hidden dignity.'

Having no doubt left the rest of the apostles on the lower slopes of the mountain, Jesus took the three up to the summit. There his clothing and his whole person, not just his face like that of Moses on Sinai, became dazzlingly white. At the same time Moses and Elijah appeared, witnesses to him from the past, and men who had suffered much and also been glorified. The end of Moses' life was shrouded in mystery, and Elijah left this earth on a heavenly chariot in a blaze of fire. St Luke reports that 'they were speaking of his passing which he was to accomplish in Jerusalem' (Luke 9.31). In his dazzling appearance they were being given a glimpse of his resurrection glory, in his association with the two prophets and in their conversation they were being showing the link between his passion and his resurrection.

Impulsively Peter asked permission to built three tents, shrines in honour of each of the three whom he now saw before them. Mark's text continues, 'And a cloud came, covering them in shadow; and there came a voice from the cloud, 'This is my Son, the Beloved. Listen to him' (Mark 9.7); Matthew's text runs, ' He was still speaking when suddenly a bright cloud covered them with shadow, and from the cloud there came a voice which said, "This is my Son, the Beloved" (Matthew 17.5).' The phrase, 'He was still speaking when ...' gives the impression that Peter's words about the tents had elicited an immediate response from the Father, who at once corrected Peter's inadequate notion of who Jesus was. Jesus was not just a third prophet alongside Moses and Elijah, but the Son of God himself.

The overshadowing by a cloud, out of which the Father's voice was heard, as was the voice of Yahweh on Sinai, relates the Transfiguration incident to the epiphany on Sinai when the law was revealed through Moses. Now the law that will be taught by the Beloved of God must command ever greater respect than the teaching given through Moses or the prophets.

As they descended from the mountain they discussed amongst themselves what 'rising from the dead' could mean. This suggests that the vision of Jesus radiant in heavenly light had started up in their minds thoughts about resurrection in general and about the resurrection of Jesus in particular. We may also surmise that, having seen the two witnesses from the past in the persons of Moses and Elijah they began to realize that their work in life was going to be to bear witness to him, whom they now knew as the beloved Son of God.

The message contained in this Gospel episode was not for the three or for the twelve alone, it is for all believers. All are called to listen to the Son of God, to his teaching as recorded in the Scriptures and as proclaimed continuously by the *magisterium* of the Church, by those who have succeeded the Twelve in the office entrusted to them by the Lord himself.

Listening manifests itself also in prayer; and it is through prayer most of all that the believer's witness become effective by his own transfiguration. In his sacred humanity Jesus himself was transfigured by prayer. In the Lucan version of the Transfiguration narrative we read: 'As *he prayed*, the aspect of his face was changed and his clothing became brilliant as lightning' (Luke 9.29).

'LISTEN TO HIM': MARK 9.2–10

Six days later, Jesus took with him Peter and James and John and led them up a high mountain where they could be alone by themselves. There in their presence he was transfigured: his clothes became dazzlingly white, whiter than any earthly bleacher could make them. Elijah appeared to them with Moses; and they were talking with Jesus. Then Peter spoke to Jesus: 'Rabbi,' he said 'it is wonderful for us to be here; so let us make three tents, one for you, one for Moses and one for Elijah'. He did not know what to say; they were so frightened. And a cloud came, covering them in shadow; and there came a voice from the cloud, 'This is my Son, the Beloved. Listen to him.' Then suddenly, when they looked round, they saw no one with them any more but only Jesus.

As they came down from the mountain he warned them to tell no one what they had seen, until after the Son of Man had risen from the dead. They observed the warning faithfully, though among themselves they discussed what 'rising from the dead' could mean.

5

The Institution of the Eucharist

The passover: Exodus 12.1–14

Yahweh said to Moses and Aaron in the land of Egypt, 'This month is to be the first of all the others for you, the first month of your year. Speak to the whole community of Israel and say, "On the tenth day of this month each man must take a animal from the flock, one for each family: one animal for each household. If the household is too small to eat the animal, a man must join with his neighbour, the nearest to his house, as the number of persons requires. You must take into account what each can eat in deciding the number for the animal. It must be an animal without blemish, a male one year old; you may take it from either sheep or goats. You must keep it till the fourteenth day of the month when the whole assembly of the community of Israel shall slaughter it between the two evenings. Some of the blood must then be taken and put on the two doorposts and the lintel of the houses where it is eaten. That night, the flesh is to be eaten, roasted over the fire; it must be eaten with unleavened bread and bitter herbs. Do not eat any of it raw or boiled, but roasted over the fire, head, feet and entrails. You must not leave any over till the morning: whatever is left till morning you are to burn. You shall eat it like this: with a girdle round your waist, sandals on your feet, a staff in your hand. You shall eat it hastily: it is a passover in honour of Yahweh. That night, I will go through the land of Egypt and strike down all the first-born in the land of Egypt, man and beast alike, and I shall deal out punishment to all the gods of Egypt. I am Yahweh! The blood shall serve to mark the houses that you live in. When I see the blood I will pass over you and you shall escape the destroying plague when I strike the land of Egypt. This day is to be a day of remembrance for you, and you must celebrate it as a feast in Yahweh's honour. For all generations you are to declare it a day of festival, for ever.'"

Covenant sacrifice and communion meal: Exodus 24.4–11

Moses put all the commands of Yahweh into writing, and early next morning he built an altar at the foot of the mountain, with twelve standing-stones for the twelve tribes of Israel. Then he directed certain young Israelites to offer holocausts and to immolate bullocks to Yahweh as communion sacrifices. Half of the blood Moses took up and put into basins, the other half he cast on the altar. And taking the Book of the Covenant he read it to the listening people, and they said, 'We will observe all that Yahweh has decreed; we will obey.' Then Moses took the blood and cast it towards the people. 'This' he said 'is the blood of the Covenant that Yahweh has made with you, containing all these rules.'

Moses went up with Aaron, Nadab and Abihu, and seventy elders of Israel. They saw the God of Israel beneath whose feet there was, it seemed, a sapphire pavement pure as the heavens themselves. He laid no hand on these notables of the sons of Israel: they gazed on God. They ate and they drank.

At table in Wisdom's house: Proverbs 9.1–5

    Wisdom has built herself a house,
       she has erected her seven pillars,
       she has slaughtered her beasts, prepared her wine,

she has laid her table.
She has despatched her maidservants
and proclaimed from the city' heights:
'Who is ignorant? Let him step this way.'
To the fool she says,
'Come and eat my bread,
drink the wine I have prepared!
Leave your folly and you will live,
walk in the ways of perception.'

The vine and its shoots: Ecclesiasticus 24.15–22
I have exhaled a perfume like cinnamon and acacia,
I have breathed out a scent like choice myrrh,
Like galbanum, onycha and stacte,
like the smoke of incense in the tabernacle.
I have spread my branches like a terebinth,
and my branches are glorious and graceful.
I am like a vine putting out graceful shoots,
my blossoms bear the fruit of glory and wealth.
Approach me, you who desire me,
and take your fill of my fruits,
for memories of me are sweeter than honey,
inheriting me is sweeter than the honeycomb.
They who eat me will hunger for more,
they who drink me will thirst for more.
Whoever listens to me will never have to blush,
whoever acts as I dictate will never sin.

The new and everlasting covenant: Hebrews 10.11–18
All the priests stand at their duties every day, offering over and over again the same sacrifices which are quite incapable of taking sins away. He, on the other hand, has offered one single sacrifice for sins, and then taken his place for ever, at the right hand of God, where he is now waiting until his enemies are made into a footstool for him. By virtue of that one single offering, he has achieved the eternal perfection of all whom he is sanctifying. The Holy Spirit assures us of this; for he says, first:

> This is the covenant I will make with them
> when those days arrive;

and the Lord then goes on to say:

> I will put my laws into their hearts
> and write them on their minds.
> I will never call their sins to mind,
> or their offences.

When all sins have been forgiven, there can be no more
sin offerings.

MEDITATION

The Mysteries of Light are introduced by the baptism of Jesus in the Jordan, an event which directs our minds towards Christian baptism, the sacrament that underlies all the other sacraments. The Mysteries of Light conclude by presenting for our meditation the sacrament of the Eucharist which lies at the centre of Christian life and worship, enabling us from time to time to breathe the air of the heavenly sanctuary

The Eucharist came as an incomparable gift from God, the sign and seal of a new covenant between God and the human race, but it is also the end-product of a long spiritual development. The Eucharist was instituted by our Lord at the celebration of his last Passover supper with the disciples, and so with good reason we conclude that the Eucharist derives from the Jewish Passover. We expect to find, therefore, an analogy between the meaning of the Passover and the meaning of the Eucharist.

What did the Passover mean to those who celebrated that festival? Year after year at the celebration of the Passover the father of the family explained to the younger generation the meaning of the festival. Eating the paschal lamb, which had been ceremonially slaughtered, commemorated the sparing the lives of the Israelites by the angel of death, who had passed over the Israelite houses when he saw the blood of the recently-slaughtered lamb smeared on the lintels and door-posts of the houses. Eating unleavened bread and bitter herbs commemorated the haste with which the Israelites fled from Egypt and were led out into the freedom of the wilderness to become the people of God.

The commentary on the Passover which the father was required to provide for his family guides our understanding of the Eucharist. Like the Passover, the Eucharist is a memorial, not now of the events which led up to and accompanied the deliverance of the Israelites from their bondage in Egypt, but of the events connected with the deliverance of the whole human race from the bondage of sin. Central in these events is the crucifixion of Jesus, the true paschal lamb, whose atoning sacrifice saves us from everlasting death. Consecrating first the bread and then the wine of the Eucharist, the priest commemorates the death of Jesus on the cross and the pouring out of his blood; then, eating the bread and drinking the wine, now the real body and blood of Christ risen from the dead, we receive into our innermost being the new life of his Spirit, and experience the joyful hope of enjoying one day the freedom of the eternal, heavenly city. In celebrating the Eucharist we pass over from death into eternal life.

The belief that the events which we commemorate in celebrating the Eucharist become really present in the celebration is consonant with the Jewish concept of a memorial, for when the Israelites celebrated the Passover they did not merely recall a past event, they experienced the power of that event, as though it were happening in the present. The Hebrew word which we translate as 'memorial' possesses this meaning of making an event present. The Church took over this Jewish concept so that, for Christians, the eucharistic memorial of our Lord's atoning sacrifice on the cross and of his rising from the dead is not just an act of mental recollection: it is a re-presentation of these acts, bringing their power into the present moment. Our Lord's sacrifice on the cross is present in every celebration of the Eucharist as truly as it was on Calvary, and the life of the Spirit increases in power in the believer who, in receiving the sacramental signs, consumes the real, risen body and blood of Christ.

The Passover is that element in Old Testament tradition

which has the most direct bearing on our understanding of the Eucharist, but it is not the only element which flows into Christian eucharistic tradition. All that the Temple stood for helps our understanding of the new covenant of reconciliation in Christ and its sealing in the mystery of the Eucharist.

The Jerusalem Temple, successor to the tabernacle of the wilderness, was a place of continuous sacrifice. Within the Temple there were countless sacrifices offered for individual sins, but most significant of all was the annual sacrifice on the Day of Atonement when the High Priest alone entered the Holy of Holies and performed the rites of atonement. A detailed description of these rites is contained in Leviticus, chapter 16. The New Testament Letter to the Hebrews sees this ritual atonement as a foreshadowing of the real atonement for the sins of mankind by our Lord Jesus, who has 'passed through the greater, the more perfect tent, which is better than the one made by men's hands because it is not of this created order; and he has entered the sanctuary once and for all, taking with him not the blood of goats and bull calves, but his own blood, having won an eternal redemption for us' (Heb. 9.11–12).

The concept of a covenant or contract being made between God and his people, and the concept of the sealing of that covenant by an outward sign, usually connected with the shedding of blood, has a very long history. In the pre-historical part of the Bible we read the tale of God's covenant with Noah, his promise that there would thereafter be stability in the functioning of the universe, the seasons would follow one another regularly, there would be no further destruction by a terrible flood; and this promise was sealed in the appearance of the rainbow. More significant, however, is the covenant made with Abraham, the seal of which was circumcision. This covenant was renewed from time to time, and its substance was always the promise God made to protect and guide his people who, for their part, promised to obey his commands. Definitive above all was the covenant made on Sinai between Yahweh and his people; and this covenant was sealed in the shedding of blood. Along with the rite of the Passover this sealing of the covenant on the slopes of Sinai provides an important Old Testament analogue of the Christian Eucharist.

The account of this Sinai covenant and its sealing is found in the book of Exodus, chapter 24, and is the first of the passages printed above. In some ways this incident is even more relevant for our understanding of the Eucharist than is the Passover. We note that young Israelites were directed to 'immolate bullocks to Yahweh as communion sacrifices'. In this incident sacrifice and communion are closely related. The bullocks are immolated as communion sacrifice, and the blood is sprinkled on the altar, representing Yahweh, and also upon the people who are thus brought into union with Yahweh and also with each other, for they are all sprinkled with the same blood. They have become the kith and kin of Yahweh and blood brothers of one another. Likewise the Eucharist is not only communion with the Lord, but also the communion of his people with one another.

A brief commentary on the Sinai covenant as recorded in Exodus chapter 24 is contained in one of the most useful books ever produced about the Old Testament: *The History of Salvation in the Old Testament* (St Paul's Publications). This quotation is from p. 137:

> The contract of the Covenant was sealed by a solemn oath of loyalty to God, based upon the Decalogue, sanctioned and consecrated by sacrifice offered with a special and clearly symbolic ceremony. The altar represents God, bestower of the Covenant; the twelve pillars represent the twelve tribes of Israel. The blood of the sacrificial victims sprinkled on the altar and the people (that is on the pillars and in the direction of those present) indicates that henceforth there is a bond, similar to the blood relationship of allied tribes, between God and the people. This Covenant is unique for in binding the people to their God; it also binds the tribes and their members to each other. On the basis of this Covenant is built the whole history of Israel. Jesus, when he instituted the Eucharist and at the

same time explained the meaning of his imminent death, referred to this episode when He said over the chalice containing the wine the words: 'This is my blood of the new covenant, which is poured out for many for the forgiveness of sins'.

After the covenant had been sealed in this fashion, the importance of communion is underlined when Moses and Aaron and Abihu along with seventy of the elders of the people go up the mountain without fear into the presence of Yahweh. They 'gazed on God. They ate and they drank' (Exodus 24.11).

The theme of communion between God and his people, of God's desire to be with his people, runs through the Old Testament in parallel to the theme of sacrifice. This theme is evident pre-eminently in the Wisdom literature. As time passed, the Wisdom of God became regarded more and more as a divine Person, and Wisdom, we are told, is 'at play every-where in the world, delighting to be with the sons of men' (Proverbs 8.31.) In the same book Wisdom is portrayed as a hostess offering lavish hospitality to her guests. She calls them to come to her table and eat bread and drink wine. The purpose of giving this food is to instil into the hearts of her guests the spirit of wisdom. Those who enjoy the meal have communion with the one who offers them hospitality: they enjoy communion with God, for the Wisdom of God is God himself. In the book of Ecclesiasticus we are told that the man who lodges close to Wisdom's house will be fed by her:

She will come to meet him like a mother,
    and receive him like a virgin bride.
She will give him the bread of understanding to eat,
    and the water of wisdom to drink. (Ecclus. 15.2–3)

In the twenty-fourth chapter of the same book the image of eating and drinking is joined with the image of the vine, an image which our Lord developed in the parable which teaches us of the substantial union of the branches with the vine-stock.

> I am like a vine putting out graceful shoots,
>   my blossoms bear the fruit of glory and wealth.
> Approach me, you who desire me,
>   and take your fill of my fruits,
> for memories of me are sweeter than honey,
>   inheriting me is sweeter than the honeycomb.
> They who eat me will hunger for more.
>   they who drink me will thirst for more.
> Whoever listens to me will never have to blush,
>   whoever acts as I dictate will never sin.
>
> (Ecclus. 24.17–22)

The two themes, atonement through sacrifice, and communion with God, which reach perfection in the Christian
Eucharist, reach far back into the tradition of Israel; and
acquaintance with that tradition helps us understand the
meaning of the Eucharist.

The Israelite sense of the real presence and action of God
in the ritual commemorations of his acts is of great importance in the Christian interpretation of the Christian ritual
commemoration of Christ's redemptive actions. Objection is
sometimes made to the notion that the sacrifice of Calvary
is re-presented in every celebration of the Eucharist, appeal
being made, for example, to Hebrews 9.12 'he has entered
the sanctuary once and for all' or to Hebrews 9.28 'Christ,
too, offers himself only once'. To apply these texts in this
way is to fail to see that they refer to our Lord's historical
sacrifice on the cross, that is to his sacrifice in time. But
Hebrews speaks also of the reality of that sacrifice within the
timelessness of the heavenly sanctuary; having entered into
the heavenly sanctuary, he 'offered himself as the perfect
sacrifice to God through the eternal Spirit' (Hebrews 9.14a).
The historical sacrifice on the cross was the ultimate manifestation in time of that sacrifice through the eternal Spirit.
The same sacrifice was made in the garden of Gethsemane,
the same sacrifice was made indeed in our Lord's initial act
of self-emptying to become man for our sakes. All of these
acts are the same sacrifice through the eternal Spirit, and

each celebration of the Eucharist is a manifestation of the sacrifice through the eternal Spirit and so is one with the sacrifice on the cross, which is that sacrifice manifested once for all in time, but which is also a sacrifice that is once and for ever.

An element in the celebration of the Eucharist which is sometimes overlooked is the contribution which the particular congregation makes to the sacrifice. Offering himself through the eternal Spirit, our Lord offers indeed the historical sacrifice of Calvary, but he takes up into his sacrifice through the eternal Spirit the offerings of those who believe in him for, as the letter to the Hebrews puts it: he 'can purify our inner self from dead actions so that we do our service to the living God' (Hebrews 9.14b). Every sacrifice of the Eucharist is a sacrifice of the whole Christ, Head and members.

This thought suggests another way of looking at the representation of Christ's sacrifice in this sacrament. The sacramental celebration not only takes us back to the cross in time, but takes us also upwards and forwards into the heavenly sanctuary. We are taken out of time into the presence of God the Father in heaven. Our celebrations of the Eucharist ought to express this fact.

Celebrating the Eucharist we are taken into the presence of God the Father in heaven; but God's presence remains with us here on earth also in the bread and wine of the Eucharist, reserved in our tabernacles. The atmosphere of heaven fills our sanctuaries just as the Shekinah hovered over the Holy of Holies in the Jerusalem Temple. Authoritative teaching about the real presence of Christ in the Eucharist was given by Christ himself, and this is recorded in the sixth chapter of St John's Gospel. Jesus said:

> I tell you most solemnly,
> if you do not eat the flesh of the Son of Man
> and drink his blood,
> you will not have life in you. (John 6.53)

Many in the crowd, even some disciples, found these words offensive, and turned away from him. Jesus did not try to gain their support by saying that his words were to be taken metaphorically, but continued in these words, which seem to contradict what he had just said:
  'What if you should see the Son of Man ascend to where he was before?

> 'It is the spirit that gives life,
> the flesh has nothing to offer.' (John 6.62)

This saying makes plain that the key to understanding the real presence of Christ in the eucharistic species is his resurrection and ascension. His dead flesh on the cross 'had nothing to offer', but having been raised from the dead by the power of the Spirit it had everything to offer. In the bread and wine of the Eucharist we eat and drink the substance into which these signs have been changed, that is the substance of the risen Christ. Our bodies consume the signs: our inner being, that in us which is destined for immortality, is nourished by the food of immortality, the substance of Christ's risen body, the substance of which restored creation will be formed. We are united with the Word and Wisdom of God; and that Word, incarnate in the Person of Christ, remains in every fragment of the elements of bread and wine in the tabernacles of our churches.

THE INSTITUTION OF THE EUCHARIST: LUKE 22.7–20

The day of Unleavened Bread came round, the day on which the passover had to be sacrificed, and [Jesus] sent Peter and John, saying, 'Go and make the preparations for us to eat the passover'. 'Where do you want us to prepare it?' they asked. 'Listen,' he said 'as you go into the city you will meet a man carrying a pitcher of water. Follow him into the house he enters and tell the owner of the house, "The Master has this to say to you: Where is the dining room in which I can eat the Passover with my disciples?" The man will show you a large upper room furnished with couches. Make the preparations there.' They set off and found everything as he had told them, and prepared the Passover.

When the hour came he took his place at table, and the apostles with him. And he said to them, 'I have longed to eat this Passover with you before I suffer; because, I tell you, I shall not eat it again until it is fulfilled in the kingdom of God.'

Then, taking a cup, he gave thanks and said,
'Take this and share it among you, because
from now on, I tell you, I shall not drink wine
until the kingdom of God comes'.
Then he took some bread, and when he had
given thanks, broke it and gave it to them,
saying, 'This is my body which will be given for
you; do this as a memorial of me'. He did the
same with the cup after supper, and said,
'This cup is the new covenant in my blood
which will be poured out for you.'

PART THREE

The Sorrowful
Mysteries

1

The Agony in the Garden

Wisdom abhors sin: Wisdom 1.4–5
   No, Wisdom will never make its way into a crafty soul
   nor stay in a body that is in debt to sin;
   the holy spirit of instruction shuns deceit,
   it stands aloof from reckless purposes,
   is taken aback when iniquity appears.

I was born guilty: Psalm 51.5–11
   You know I was born guilty,
   a sinner from the moment of conception.

   Yet, since you love sincerity of heart,
   teach me the secrets of wisdom.
   Purify me with hyssop until I am clean;
   wash me until I am whiter than snow.

   Instil some joy and gladness into me,
   let the bones you have crushed rejoice again.
   hide your face from my sins,
   wipe out all my guilt.

   God, create a clean heart in me,
   put into me a new and constant spirit,
   do not banish me from your presence,
   do not deprive me of your holy spirit.

A priest for ever: Hebrews 7.11–19; 26–8

Now if perfection had been reached through the levitical priesthood because the Law given to the nation rests on it, why was it still necessary for a new priesthood to arise, one of the same order as Melchizedek not counted as being 'of the same order as' Aaron? But any change in the priesthood must mean a change in the Law as well.

So our Lord, of whom these things were said, belonged to a different tribe, the members of which have never done service at the altar; everyone knows he came from Judah, a tribe which Moses did not even mention when dealing with priests.

This becomes even more clearly evident when there appears a second Melchizedek, who is a priest not by virtue of a law about physical descent, but by the power of an indestructible life. For it was about him that the prophecy was made: You are a priest of the order of Melchizedek, and for ever. The earlier commandment is thus abolished, because it was neither effective nor useful, since the Law could not make anyone perfect; but now this commandment is replaced by something better – the hope that brings us nearer to God.

To suit us, the ideal high priest would have to be holy, innocent and uncontaminated, beyond the influence of sinners, and raised up above the heavens; one who would not need to offer sacrifices every day, as the other high priests do for their own sins and then for those of the people, because he has done this once and for all by offering himself. The Law appoints high priests who are men subject to weakness; but the promise on oath, which came after the Law, appointed the Son who is made perfect for ever.

The inward struggle: Romans 7.21–5

In fact, this seems to be the rule, that every single time I want to do good it is something evil that comes to hand. In my inmost self I dearly love God's Law, but I can see that my body follows a different law that battles against the law of sin which my reason dictates. This is what makes me a prisoner of that law which lives inside my body.

What a wretched man I am! Who will rescue me from this body doomed to death? Thanks be to God through Jesus Christ our Lord!

In short, it is I who with my reason serve the Law of God, and no less I who serve in my unspiritual self the law of sin.

'Now my soul is troubled': John 12.23–8
Jesus replied to them:
  'Now the hour has come
  for the Son of Man to be glorified.
  I tell you, most solemnly,
  unless a wheat grain falls on the ground and dies,
  it remains only a single grain;
  but if it dies,
  it yields a rich harvest.
  Anyone who loves his life loses it;
  anyone who hates his life in this world
  will keep it for the eternal life.
  If a man serves me, he must follow me,
  wherever I am, my servant will be there too.
  If anyone serves me, my Father will honour him.
  Now my soul is troubled.
  What shall I say:
  Father, save me from this hour?
  But it was for this very reason that I have come to
    this hour.
  Father, glorify your name!'
  A voice came from heaven, 'I have glorified it, and I
    will glorify it again'.

MEDITATION

The five joyful mysteries of the Rosary, based upon the first two chapters of St Luke's Gospel, have provided us with very much more than a superficial historical record of our Lord's birth and growing up. They contain a profound theological statement about who our Lord really is, an adumbration of his atoning sacrifice, and they give us a glimpse of his victory and enduring presence on earth in his new people. The infancy narrative and the Rosary mysteries based upon it are, indeed, a statement of the whole framework of the story of salvation, with special emphasis laid not upon our Lord's humanity, as we might have expected in an infancy story, but upon the mystery of his divinity.

The Mysteries of Light, the chaplet which has been recently added by Pope John Paul II to the original three, likewise present an overall picture of the mystery of salvation, beginning with the baptism of our Lord, when he identified himself with sinful humanity and the mystery of the Blessed Trinity was revealed, and ending with the great mystery of his enduring presence in the sacrament of the Holy Eucharist.

In the five Sorrowful Mysteries we focus our attention upon the details of the last week of our Lord's life on earth, the events we commemorate annually in Holy Week. There is a logical link between the fifth Joyful Mystery and the first Sorrowful Mystery, and this is expressed in the biblical text quoted at the end of the fifth Joyful Mystery: 'You prepared a body for me, I said "God, here I am! I am coming to obey your will"'. The theme of this mystery is the conflict between the spirit and the flesh, the flesh which for our sakes the Lord took from the Virgin Mary. In his human nature our Lord endured the agonizing conflict which can arise out of one's knowing God's will and being at the same time subject to the body's powerful natural instinct for self preservation. In this conflict, Jesus was victorious; he overcame the frailty inherent in his human nature and, with a perfect heart, sacrificed his body because that was what God the Father commanded him to do.

In recounting this incident, St Luke, who in his infancy story had been at pains to use all his literary talent to stress the divinity of Christ, takes trouble now to stress the reality of Christ's conflict and human agony. He of all the evangelists says that an angel came to give our Lord strength. Just as men cry out in such a trial for some supernatural assistance, so our Lord was human enough to have to cry out in like manner. And Luke also tells us that 'his sweat fell to the ground like great drops of blood'. In this way he underlines the reality of our Lord's agony.

The three evangelists, Matthew, Mark and Luke, bring out the reality of the agony in another way. All link the scene with the foretelling of Peter's denial, when he, after thrice being put to the test, would persist in disclaiming all knowledge of Jesus; and all three include in the agony scene our Lord's admonition to the disciples to 'Pray not to be put to the test'. Our Lord is comparing his own testing here with the kind of testing that is bound to come upon his disciples. It is no less real a testing for him than it will be for them, and he too must resort to the only aid available: prayer to his heavenly Father. The evangelists are telling us that our Lord's divinity did not cause his testing to be less than that which men from time to time endure.

They suggest, indeed, that it was much more. Matthew and Mark say that Jesus took Peter and James and John aside with him to be witnesses of his agony, just as he had taken them to be witnesses of his transfiguration. The implied contrast between the two scenes suggests that as the former had been unspeakable in splendour so the latter was unutterable in horror. Being joined with divinity did not deprive our Lord's humanity of its natural sensitivity to suffering. The very opposite was true. The knowledge Christ had as God was what gave rise to the intensity of his agony. He knew exactly what was about to happen to him, and could fathom, as no man could ever fathom, the mysterious horror of being saddled with the sin of the whole world. He was about to go down and perform the spiritual equivalent of cleaning out a cesspool with his bare hands. In some sense, which baffles the mind of man, he was about to come so closely in contact with sin as to take upon himself the blame for all the ugliest and meanest things that have ever been done or ever will be done until the end of the world. As St Paul puts it 'He was made sin for us' (2 Corinthians 5.21). This was a horror that God alone could fully appreciate, and our Lord faced it and accepted it. And so, St Luke tells us, when he returned from his agony, having decided to go through with all that lay ahead, he found the disciples 'sleeping from sheer grief'. They had been unable to look on at his suffering.

Finding the disciples asleep, Jesus roused them with the words: 'You can sleep on now and take your rest. It is all over' (Mark 14.41). He had no further need of their spasmodic and unreliable prayers, for his victory was won. The words, 'It is all over', remind us of Jesus' last words from the cross (John 19.30): 'It is accomplished'. Perhaps the climax of our Lord's passion was his agony in the garden. There, by reason of his divine foreknowledge, he endured all his physical sufferings in advance, along with the mental agony of his spiritual association with the sin of the world. The decision made then, to drink the cup of suffering offered him by his Father in heaven, was his victory.

If we see our Lord's passion and victory over sin primarily in the interior submission of his will, which reached a climax in the agony in the garden, we find it easier to understand the relationship between the sacrifice once offered upon the cross and the sacrifice renewed all down the ages upon the altar in the celebration of the Holy Eucharist. Both cross and Eucharist are external manifestations of an interior sacrifice of will, of the infinite and eternal mediation of Christ the high priest who has entered into the heavenly sanctuary, having first 'offered himself as the perfect sacrifice to God through the eternal Spirit'. The efficacy of the cross is presented eternally by the great high priest in the heavenly sanctuary; the Church joins her offering with that eternal presentation, and so with the efficacy of the cross, every time she offers the consecrated bread and wine in the sacrifice of the Mass. Christ's historical sacrifice was unique, once for all, but his sacrifice is also one in eternity. Christ's sacrifice, perpetually presented before the Father in heaven, continually descends with power to earth, like great drops of blood falling to the ground.

AGONY IN THE GARDEN OF GETHSEMANE: MARK 14.32–42

*They came to a small estate called Gethsemane,
and Jesus said to his disciples, 'Stay here while
I pray'. Then he took Peter and James and
John with him. And a sudden fear came over
him, and great distress. And he said to them,
'My soul is sorrowful to the point of death.
Wait here, and keep awake.' And going on a
little further he threw himself on the ground
and prayed that, if it were possible, this hour
might pass him by. 'Abba (Father)!' he said
'Everything is possible for you. Take this cup
away from me. But let it be as you, not I,
would have it.' He came back and found them
sleeping, and he said to Peter, 'Simon, are you
asleep? Had you not the strength to keep awake
one hour? You should be awake, and praying
not to be put to the test. The spirit is willing,
but the flesh is weak.' Again he went away and
prayed, saying the same words. And once more
he came back and found them sleeping, their
eyes were so heavy; and they could find no
answer for him. He came back a third time and*

said to them, 'You can sleep on now and take
your rest. It is all over. The hour has come.
Now the Son of Man is to be betrayed into the
hands of sinners. Get up! Let us go! My
betrayer is close at hand already.'

2

The Scourging at the Pillar

The pride of the sensualist: Wisdom 2.6–20
 'Come then, let us enjoy what good things there are,
 use this creation with the zest of youth:
 take our fill of the dearest wines and perfumes,
 let not one flower of springtime pass us by,
 before they wither crown ourselves with roses.
 Let none of us forgo his part in our orgy,
 let us leave the signs of our revelry everywhere,
 this is our portion, this the lot assigned us.

 'As for the virtuous man who is poor, let us oppress
   him;
 let us not spare the widow,
 nor respect old age, white-haired with many years.
 Let our strength be the yardstick of virtue,
 since weakness argues its own futility.
 Let us lie in wait for the virtuous man, since he annoys
   us,
 and opposes our way of life,
 reproaches us for our breaches of the law
 and accuses us of playing false to our upbringing.
 He claims to have knowledge of God,
 and calls himself a son of the Lord.
 Before us he stands, a reproof to our way of thinking,

the very sight of him weighs our spirits down;
his way of life is not like other men's,
the paths he treads are unfamiliar.
In his opinion we are counterfeit;
he holds aloof from our doings as though from filth;
he proclaims the final end of the virtuous as happy
and boasts of having God for his father.
Let us see if what he says is true,
let us observe what kind of end he himself will have.
If the virtuous man is God's son, God will take his part
and rescue him from the clutches of his enemies.
Let us test him with cruelty and torture,
and thus explore this gentleness of his
and put his endurance to the proof.
Let us condemn him to a shameful death
since he will be looked after – we have his word for it.'

The suffering servant of God: Isaiah 50.4–9
The Lord Yahweh has given me
a disciple's tongue.
So that I may know how to reply to the wearied
he provides me with speech.
Each morning he wakes me to hear,
to listen like a disciple.
The Lord Yahweh has opened my ear.

For my part I made no resistance,
neither did I turn away.
I offered my back to those who struck me,
my cheeks to those who tore at my beard;
I did not cover my face
against insult and spittle.

The Lord Yahweh comes to my help,
so that I am untouched by the insults.
So, too, I set my face like flint;
I know I shall not be shamed.

My vindicator is here at hand. Does anyone start
   proceedings against me?
Then let us go to court together.
Who thinks he has a case against me?
Let him approach me.
The Lord Yahweh is coming to my help,
who dare condemn me?
They shall all go to pieces like a garment
devoured by moths.

The sacred pillar of idolatry: Judges 6.25–30
Now that night Yahweh said to Gideon, 'Take your
father's fattened calf, and pull down the altar to Baal
belonging to your father and cut down the sacred post at
the side of it. Then, on top of this bluff, build a carefully-
constructed altar to Yahweh your God. Then take the
fattened calf and burn it as a holocaust on the wood of the
sacred post you have cut down.' Then Gideon chose ten
of his servants and did as Yahweh had ordered him. But
since he stood too much in fear of his family and the
townspeople to do this by day, he did it by night. Next
morning, when the townspeople got up, the altar to Baal
had been destroyed, the sacred post that had stood beside
it was now cut down, and the fattened calf had been burnt
as a holocaust on the newly-built altar. Then they said to
each other, 'Who has done this?' They searched, made
enquiries and declared, 'Gideon son of Joash has done it'
Then the townspeople said to Joash, 'Bring out your son
for he must die, since he has destroyed the altar to Baal
and cut down the sacred post that stood beside it'.

Divine truth given up for a lie: Romans 1.18–52
The anger of God is being revealed from heaven against
all the impiety and depravity of men who keep truth
imprisoned in their wickedness. For what can be known
about God is perfectly plain to them since God himself has
made it plain. Ever since God created the world his everlasting power and deity – however invisible – have been

there for the mind to see in the things he has made. That is why such people are without excuse: they knew God and yet refused to honour him as God or to thank him; instead, they made nonsense out of logic and their empty minds were darkened. The more they called themselves philosophers, the more stupid they grew, until they exchanged the glory of the immortal God for a worthless imitation, for the image of mortal man, of birds, of quadrupeds and reptiles. That is why God left them to their filthy enjoyments and the practices with which they dishonour their own bodies, since they have given up divine truth for a lie and have worshipped and served creatures instead of the creator, who is blessed for ever. Amen!

Hated for belonging to me: John 15.18–23
    'If the world hates you,
    remember that it hated me before you.
    If you belonged to the world,
    the world would love you as its own;
    but because you do not belong to the world,
    because my choice withdrew you from the world,
    therefore the world hates you.
    Remember the words I said to you:
    A servant is not greater than his master.
    If they persecuted me,
    they will persecute you too;
    if they kept my word,
    they will keep yours as well.
    But it will be on my account that they will do all this,
    because they do not know the one who sent me.
    If I had not come,
    if I had not spoken to them,
    they would have been blameless;
    but as it is they have no excuse for their sin.
    Anyone who hates me hates my Father.'

MEDITATION

The scourging of our Lord is the culmination of a sequence of events: his arrest in the garden, his trial before the Jewish court, and his trial before two secular courts. The scourging is the first expression of sinful mankind's judgement of the sinless Son of God. Behind the horror of the action, therefore, is the appalling situation which made it possible: darkness is displacing light, justice is being utterly perverted, truth is being made to stand upon its head, man is imputing to One who is sinless, all those sins of which he himself is guilty. Man is changing places with God.

In the third chapter of his Gospel, St John reports our Lord's saying: 'Everybody who does wrong hates the light and avoids it, for fear his actions should be exposed'. The scene upon which we now meditate begins at the dead of night. Guided by Judas, the Temple guard set out under cover of darkness to arrest Jesus. To justify their action, the Temple authorities have to pretend that they are out to apprehend a dangerous political agitator, although in all his teaching, Jesus had insisted that he had no political ambitions at all. This insistence was summed up in his reply to Pilate: 'Mine is not a kingdom of this world; if my kingdom were of this world, my men would have fought to prevent my being surrendered to the Jews.' And so, as the guard approach to take him, Jesus reproves both the absurdity and the hypocrisy of their action in the words: 'Am I a brigand that you had to set out with swords and clubs? When I was among you in the Temple day after day you never moved to lay hands on me. But this is your hour; this is the reign of darkness'. The hypocrisy of Jesus' accusers reaches its climax when, in response to Pilate's offer to release Jesus, they demand the release of Barabbas, whose crime was the very one they pretended to abhor: insurrection against the Romans.

Before taking Jesus to the Roman court of justice, however, where they brought this accusation of inciting the mob to revolt, they took him to the supreme Jewish court, the Sanhedrin. In this court false witnesses were procured in an attempt to convict Jesus of blasphemy. This was another piece of quite unnecessary perjury, for Jesus was perfectly willing to admit to what the authorities assumed was blasphemy. The high priest asked: 'Are you the Christ, the Son of the Blessed One?' Jesus answered simply: 'I am', thus using the name of God himself. Hearing this, the high priest tore his robes and shouted out: 'What need have we of witnesses now?' Their minds were made up. He was to die, whatever means had to be employed to accomplish that end.

The violent rejection of Jesus' claim to be the Son of God, by the custodians of the ancient revelation of God, is one of the saddest themes in the Gospels. It is developed throughout St John's Gospel, in elaboration of his announcement in the Prologue that 'He came to his own domain and his own people did not accept him'. Not that all of his own people rejected him. We have already noted in the Joyful Mysteries how the devout mind, formed by the Old Testament in people like Simeon, the shepherds, and Joseph and Mary, was perfectly adapted to grasp the meaning of this new and perfect revelation, and to adore the Word made flesh; but the official custodians of the Old Testament revelation seemed, by contrast, to be of all men the least able to see the glory of God in Jesus Christ. This blindness is portrayed by the evangelists as more than a mere disability: it is culpable wickedness. Our Lord said:

If I had not come,
if I had not spoken to them,

they would have been blameless;
but as it is they have no excuse for their sin.
Anyone who hates me hates my Father.
If I had not performed such works among them
as no one else has ever done,
they would be blameless,
but as it is, they have seen all this,
and still they hate both me and my Father. (John 15.22–4)

The Jewish rulers' attack on Jesus was allegedly a defence of the transcendence of God the Father. The evangelists, St John in particular, declare that any man who really knew the Father and his deeds, and who possessed a genuine understanding of the Old Testament, which was the chief means of acquiring such knowledge, would recognize the acts of the Father in the actions of Jesus, and thus be led to accept the mystery of his oneness with the Father. The rulers do not know Jesus because they do not know the Father. Their theology is merely theoretical, a matter of words, and so, in their ignorance, they seek to vindicate the Father's transcendence by convicting the Son of blasphemy.

The scene now shifts to the Roman court. The Gospels give more than a hint that Pontius Pilate, the governor, was impressed with Jesus and wanted to acquit him. First he told the Jews that it was their own domestic affair, and they should try Jesus according to their law. This did not satisfy the Jewish leaders, for they were not allowed to put a man to death and so, suspecting that Pilate 'realised that it was out of jealousy that the chief priests had handed Jesus over' (Mark 15.10), they then began to press the charge of sedition. Pilate tried to sidestep the issue by offering to release Jesus according to the Passover custom of granting political amnesty to one prisoner. Finally the Jewish leaders put pressure on Pilate by hinting that Rome would be displeased with him if there was an uproar. In effect they told Pilate that it was as much as his job was worth if he did not accede to their request. And so Pilate gave in, knowing that he became accessory to a great crime, but too weak to stand up for the truth. His question: 'What is truth?' was a pathetic attempt to plead philosophical scepticism in mitigation of his perfidy.

By a strange irony Pilate's attempt to avoid the issue, by having Jesus scourged in the hope that this might satisfy the chief priests, set Jesus in immediate association with a symbol of human weakness and sensuality. The pillar to which Jesus was bound is reminiscent of the sacred pillar of ancient Canaanite worship. The fact that the pillar persists in the traditional imagination of the Church, although it is not mentioned explicitly by the evangelists, may be an indication of its primeval significance for human consciousness. The sacred pillar was a phallic symbol forming part of the apparatus of the cruel and sensual worship that went on at the local shrines in the 'high places' in Palestine before the Israelites conquered the land. Indeed, it continued after that time, for it was one of these pillars that Gideon chopped down and burned in defiance of the local gods. This ritual object, like the sacred prostitutes, who were another feature of the Canaanite cults, reminds us of the sensuality and vice that are the soil of idolatrous pactice.

This scene in the Gospel story ends, therefore, not only in terrible physical torture, but in abominable humiliation: the fountain of holiness is bound to an ancient symbol of blatant idolatry. Thus humiliated, he takes upon his flesh the punishment for all the sins of human viciousness and sensuality.

JESUS IS SCOURGED: MARK 15.1–15

First thing in the morning, the chief priests together with the elders and scribes, in short the whole Sanhedrin, had their plan ready. They had Jesus bound and took him away and handed him over to Pilate.
Pilate questioned him, 'Are you the king of the Jews?' 'It is you who say it' he answered. And the chief priests brought many accusations against him. Pilate questioned him again, 'Have you no reply at all? See how many accusations they are bringing against you!' But, to Pilate's amazement, Jesus made no further reply.
At festival time Pilate used to release a prisoner for them, anyone they asked for. Now a man called Barabbas was then in prison with the rioters who had committed murder during the uprising. When the crowd went up and began to ask Pilate the customary favour, Pilate answered them, 'Do you want me to release for you the king of the Jews?' For he realised it was out of jealousy that the chief

priests had handed Jesus over. The chief priests, however, had incited the crowd to demand that he should release Barabbas for them instead. Then Pilate spoke again. 'But in that case,' he said to them, 'what am I to do with the man you call king of the Jews?' They shouted back, 'Crucify him!' 'Why?' Pilate asked them, 'What harm has he done?' But they shouted all the louder, 'Crucify him!' So Pilate, anxious to placate the crowd, released Barabbas for them and, having ordered Jesus to be scourged, handed him over to be crucified.

3

The Crowning with Thorns

Wretched, slowly dying: Psalm 88.8–14
 You have turned my friends against me
  and made me repulsive to them;
 in prison and unable to escape,
  my eyes are worn out with suffering.

 Yahweh, I invoke you all day,
  I stretch out my hands to you:
 are your marvels meant for the dead,
  can ghosts rise up to praise you?

 Who talks of your love in the grave,
  of your faithfulness in the place of perdition?
 Do they hear about your marvels in the dark,
  About your righteousness in the land of oblivion?

 But I am here, calling for your help,
  praying to you every morning:
 why do you reject me?
  Why do you hide your face from me?

The innocent sufferer: Job 13.23–8
 How many faults and crimes have I committed?
  What law have I transgressed, or in what have I
  offended?

Why do you hide your face
  and look on me as your enemy?
Will you intimidate a wind-blown leaf,
  will you chase the dried-up chaff;
you list bitter accusations against me,
  taxing me with the faults of my youth,
after putting my feet in the stocks,
  watching my every step,
  and measuring my footprints;
while my life is crumbling like rotten wood,
  or a moth-eaten garment.

A daily laughing-stock: Jeremiah 20.7–10
  You have seduced me, Yahweh, and I have let myself
    be seduced;
  you have overpowered me: you were the stronger.
  I am a daily laughing-stock,
  everybody's butt.
  Each time I speak the word, I have to howl
  and proclaim: 'Violence and ruin!'
  The word of Yahweh has meant for me
  insult, derision, all day long.
  I used to say, 'I will not think about him,
  I will not speak in his name any more'.
  Then there seemed to be a fire burning in my heart,
  imprisoned in my bones.
  The effort to restrain it wearied me,
  I could not bear it.
  I hear so many disparaging me,
  '"Terror from every side!"
  Denounce him! Let us denounce him!'
  All those who used to be my friends
  watched for my downfall,
  'Perhaps he will be seduced into error.
  Then we will master him
  and take our revenge!'

The man we used to laugh at: Wisdom 5.4–5
   'This is the man we used to laugh at once,
   a butt for our sarcasm, fools that we were!
   His life we regarded as madness,
   his ending as without honour.
   How has he come to be counted as one of the sons
      of God?
   How does he come to be assigned a place among
      the saints?'

The imitation of Christ: Acts 25.23–7; 26.24–32)
So the next day Agrippa and Bernice arrived in great
state and entered the audience chamber attended by the
tribunes and the city notables; and Festus ordered Paul to
be brought in. Then Festus said, 'King Agrippa, and all
here present with us, you see before you the man about
whom the whole Jewish community has petitioned me,
both in Jerusalem and here, loudly protesting that he
ought not to be allowed to remain alive. For my own part
I am satisfied that he has committed no capital crime, but
when he himself appealed to the august emperor I
decided to send him. But I have nothing definite that I
can write to his Imperial Majesty about him; that is why I
have produced him before you all, and before you in
particular, King Agrippa, so that after the examination I
may have something to write. It seems to me pointless to
send a prisoner without indicating the charges against
him.'
   Then Agrippa said to Paul, 'You have leave to speak on
your own behalf'. And Paul held up his hand and began
his defence:
   [*There follows, in chapter 26, Paul's defence which is an
example of the* kerygma *or proclamation of the Christian gospel.
Chapter 26 ends with an account of the hearers' reactions to this
preaching.*]
   He had reached this point in his defence when Festus
shouted out, 'Paul, you are out of your mind; all that learning of yours is driving you mad'. 'Festus, your Excellency,'

answered Paul 'I am not mad: I am speaking nothing but the sober truth. The king understands these matters, and to him I now speak with assurance, confident that nothing of all this is lost on him; after all, these things were not done in a corner. King Agrippa, do you believe in the prophets? I know you do.' At this Agrippa said to Paul, 'A little more, and your arguments would make a Chrisian of me'. 'Little or more,' Paul replied 'I wish before God that not only you but all who have heard me today would come to be as I am – except for these chains.'

At this the king rose to his feet, with the governor and Bernice and those who sat there with them. When they had retired they talked together and agreed, 'This man is doing nothing that deserves death or imprisonment'. And Agrippa remarked to Festus, 'The man could have been set free if he had not appealed to Caesar'.

MEDITATION

The crowning with thorns is closely connected with the scourging at the pillar. The crowning with thorns and clothing in purple is like the insult that is added to an injury, although, as we saw, the scourging was itself a deep and cruel insult, and the crowning with thorns, although meant primarily as mockery, was also a severe torture. The crowning with thorns, however, is the appropriate climax to a particular idea which runs through the trial before Pilate. In handing Jesus over to Pilate for trial, the Sanhedrin were presenting him in the role of a political Messiah, as a national hero, come to free his people from the Roman yoke. Some among the Jews may have shared in this expectation; others may have been quite happy to leave things as they were and enjoy their privileged position under Roman patronage. Whatever their private views, all agreed that to portray this man Jesus as one claiming to be the popular Messiah was the best way to discredit him with the Roman authorities. Pilate could scarcely ignore the charge.

The idea seemed to grip Pilate's imagination. His first question was 'Are you the king of the Jews?'; and all through the trial, Pilate kept coming back to the concept of kingship, as if, by some mysterious enlightenment, he were beginning to see the deeper meaning of the word, and almost to believe that the description might be accurate. Pilate's preoccupation with the phrase 'king of the Jews' is betrayed also by his sarcastic comment, 'Do you want me to crucify your king?', and by his stubborn refusal to alter the superscription on the cross. When the chief priests complained of the title, 'King of the Jews,' Pilate answered testily, 'What I have written, I have written', his one feeble attempt to stand up to the Jewish Sanhedrin.

The crowning with thorns and the clothing in purple is thus a sign of the rejection by both the Jews and the Roman soldiers of the kingship of Christ. To the eye of pride and cruelty, Jesus appeared as an object of contempt: a half-dead human being, dressed up in royal purple, a diadem of sharp thorns on his head, and a reed for a sceptre in his hand; but to the eye of faith he appears as the 'lamb of God that takes away the sin of the world', the world's true king.

St Luke introduces an interesting variation into this part of the Gospel story. He does not mention the scourging or the crowning directly, but his reticence is most effective. Having described the anger of the mob, and told us that in the end Pilate yielded to their demand, he adds the terse and ominous comment that Pilate 'handed Jesus over to them to deal with as they pleased', leaving us with the picture of a crowd hungry for sadistic pleasure.

Luke includes also material that is absent from the other three evangelists. He reports that Pilate, discovering Jesus to be a Galilean, tried to pass responsibility over to Herod Antipas, the tetrarch of Galilee. This action introduces another social group. Herod was one of the native puppet rulers. He was a Jew, but one who had become Hellenized; that is, he sat loosely to the tradition of his fathers, having succumbed to the allurements of pagan Greek culture. He was a man of the world. We meet him earlier in the Gospel story as the man rebuked by John the Baptist for adultery with his brother's wife, and who then had John the Baptist beheaded. We learn, too, (Matt. 14.1–2) that he thought Jesus might be John the Baptist come back from the dead, and he was very anxious to see a miracle. His pleasure now at seeing Jesus for himself was completely insincere and worldly. In Herod, our Lord faced the world and Satan and all his empty promises. Herod represented the kind of worldliness and sensuality that was symbolized in the sacred pillar of Canaanite worship, for he was typical of the Jew who had accommodated himself to the world's idolatry. Herod's response to our Lord, in keeping with the frivolity of his life, was contempt and mockery. He had Jesus dressed up in a prince's cloak, ironically acknowledging him as the prince of David's line.

St Luke tells how on that day Herod and Pilate were reconciled, having previously been enemies. In the Acts of the Apostles, written also by Luke, he refers to this incident, seeing it as the fulfilment of a prophecy in Psalm 2.1–2:

'Kings on earth setting out to war,
princes making an alliance,
against the Lord and against his Anointed.' (Acts 4.26)

An even more significant link between St Luke's Gospel and the book of Acts is the parallel between the record of the passion of our Lord and the story of St Paul's arrest and trials, recorded at length from chapter 21 of Acts onwards.

The passion story had begun in the Temple, where Jesus taught daily in the days immediately preceding his arrest. His claim to be able to destroy the Temple and rebuild it in three days, and his driving out of those whose job was to change all foreign currency into the Temple coinage were correctly interpreted by the chief priests as an attack upon what the Temple represented, viz., the exclusiveness and finality of the Jewish law and religion. In Acts 21 St Paul is portrayed in the same role. He is accused of bringing Greeks into the Temple, a violation of Jewish exclusiveness, and in general of preaching everywhere 'against the Law and against this place'. The accusation is a recapitulation of the charge the Sanhedrin had made against Jesus. Paul was announcing the limited scope of the Jewish faith, and pointing to its perfection in the Gospel of the resurrection of Christ. It was because the chief priests and their followers refused to admit this need for fulfilment that they were moved to such fury against both Jesus and Paul.

And so St Paul suffers the same fate as his Master, even to the detail of the slap on the face (Acts 23.2). The mob clamour for his death. The Roman police arrest him and he begins a long period of trial and captivity. The series of trials to which he is subjected before the Sanhedrin, Pilate, and Agrippa, reminds us of the trials of Jesus. The different groups play roughly the same parts: the Sanhedrin persist in demanding the death penalty; the Romans, afraid of the Jews, keep Paul prisoner, although convinced of his innocence; Agrippa, the Jewish puppet ruler, takes an academic and supercilious interest in the prisoner.

It is the interlude at Caesarea, where Paul appears before the local ruler King Agrippa II, that gives the story a clear affinity with Luke's Gospel. Agrippa was grand-nephew of Herod Antipas of the Gospel story. Like his great-uncle, Agrippa represents the 'sophisticated' world, the people who often find religion 'interesting,' but are ruled, not by its precepts, but by their own inclinations.

Footnote 'e' to chapter 25 of Acts in the Jerusalem Bible gives a hint of the kind of people Agrippa and his sister Bernice were.*

The story of St Paul's arrest and imprisonment reveals the truth of our Lord's saying: 'The disciple is not above his master'. It is in miniature the story of the Church and of every Christian. Paul had already set foot on the way of the cross, had begun to suffer in the same way and for exactly the same reasons as his Master; but his road to Calvary, like the road taken by most Christians, was to stretch out over many years, in the course of which he was to be given many opportunities of preaching the Gospel. We notice too that at his several trials St Paul's audience were always divided. The chief priests condemned him, some of the Pharisees showed sympathy; Felix, the Roman governor, was divided

* Agrippa, Bernice and Drusilla were children of Herod Agrippa I. The eldest, later Agrippa II, was born in 27. At this time Bernice was living with her brother and their relationship became matter for gossip; some years later Bernice became the mistress of Titus, the Roman general, later emperor.

in his own mind: he listened attentively, but closed his ears to the message when it began to touch him on the raw; Herod Agrippa, in a tentative way, said: 'A little more, and your arguments would make a Christian of me'. In the end it is not Jesus or Paul or any of the Lord's disciples who are on trial, but those to whom their message is declared. Every believer shares in the kingship of Christ, and is a member of the new royal and priestly kingdom, enjoying the supreme dignity of those who suffer for the truth's sake. Only those who are on the side of truth listen to the voice of Christ and of those who preach in his name.

A PURPLE ROBE AND A CROWN OF THORNS: MARK 15.16–20

The soldiers led him away to the inner part of the palace, that is, the Praetorium, and called the whole cohort together. They dressed him up in purple, twisted some thorns into a crown and put it on him. And they began saluting him, 'Hail, king of the Jews!' They struck his head with a reed and spat on him; and they went down on their knees to do him homage. And when they had finished making fun of him, they took off the purple and dressed him in his own clothes.

4

Our Lord carries the Cross

The sacrifice of Isaac: Genesis 22.1–14
It happened some time later that God put Abraham to the
test. 'Abraham, Abraham' he called. 'Here I am' he
replied. 'Take your son,' God said 'your only child Isaac,
whom you love, and go to the land of Moriah. There you
shall offer him as a burnt offering, on a mountain I will
point out to you.'

Rising early next morning Abraham saddled his ass and
took with him two of his servants and his son Isaac. He
chopped wood for the burnt offering and started on his
journey to the place God had pointed out to him. On the
third day Abraham looked up and saw the place in the
distance. Then Abraham said to his servants, 'Stay here
with the donkey. The boy and I will go over there; we will
worship and come back to you.'

Abraham took the wood for the burnt offering, loaded
it on Isaac, and carried in his own hands the fire and the
knife. Then the two of them set out together. Isaac spoke
to his father Abraham. 'Father' he said. 'Yes, my son' he
replied. 'Look,' he said, 'here are the fire and the wood,
but where is the lamb for the burnt offering?' Abraham
answered, 'My son, God himself will provide the lamb for
the burnt offering'. Then the two of them went on
together.

When they arrived at the place God had pointed out to him, Abraham built an altar there, and arranged the wood. Then he bound his son Isaac and put him on the altar on top of the wood. Abraham stretched out his hand and seized the knife to kill his son.

But the angel of Yahweh called to him from heaven. 'Abraham, Abraham' he said. 'I am here' he replied. 'Do not raise your hand against the boy' the angel said. 'Do not harm him, for now I know you fear God. You have not refused me your son, your only son.' Then looking up, Abraham saw a ram caught by its horns in a bush. Abraham took the ram and offered it as a burnt offering in place of his son.

Slave-driven: Exodus 5.10–14

The people's slave-drivers went out with the overseers to speak to the people. 'Pharaoh has given orders' they said: ' "I will not provide you with straw. Go out and collect straw for yourselves wherever you can find it. But your output is not to be any less." ' So the people scattered all over the land of Egypt to gather stubble for making chopped straw. The slave-drivers harassed them. 'Every day you must complete your daily quota,' they said 'just as you did when straw was provided for you.' And the foremen who had been appointed for the sons of Israel by Pharaoh's slave-drivers were flogged, and they were asked, 'Why have you not produced your full amount of bricks as before, either yesterday or today?'

'Let me sink no further': Psalm 69.13–21

> For my part, I pray to you, Yahweh,
>   at the time you wish;
> in your great love, answer me, God,
> faithful in saving power.

> Pull me out of this swamp; let me sink no further,
>   let me escape those who hate me,
>   save me from deep water!

Do not let the waves wash over me,
     do not let the deep swallow me
or the Pit close its mouth on me.

In your loving kindness, answer me, Yahweh,
in your great tenderness turn to me;
do not hide your face from your servant,
quick, I am in trouble, answer me;
come to my side, redeem me,
from so many enemies ransom me.

You know all the insults I endure,
every one of my oppressors is known to you;
the insults have broken my heart,
my shame and disgrace are past cure;
I had hoped for sympathy, but in vain,
I found no one to console me.

They gave me poison to eat instead,
when I was thirsty they gave me vinegar to drink.

Christ has entered the sanctuary: Hebrews 9.11–14
But now Christ has come, as the high priest of all the
blessings which were to come. He has passed through the
greater, the more perfect tent, which is better than the
one made by men's hands because it is not of this created
order; and he has entered the sanctuary once and for all,
taking with him not the blood of goats and bull calves, but
his own blood, having won an eternal redemption for us.
The blood of goats and bulls and the ashes of a heifer are
sprinkled on those who have incurred defilement and
they restore the holiness of their outward lives; how much
more effectively the blood of Christ, who offered himself
as the perfect sacrifice to God through the eternal Spirit,
can purify our inner self from dead actions so that we do
our service to the living God.

Those who judge will be judged: Romans 2.1–11
So no matter who you are, if you pass judgement you
have no excuse. In judging others you condemn yourself,

since you behave no differently from those you judge. We know that God condemns that sort of behaviour impartially: and when you judge those who behave like this while you are doing exactly the same, do you think you will escape God's judgement? Or are you abusing his abundant goodness, patience and toleration, not realising that this goodness of God is meant to lead you to repentance? Your stubborn refusal to repent is only adding to the anger God will have towards you on that day of anger when his just judgements will be made known. He will repay each one as his works deserve. For those who sought renown and honour and immortality by always doing good there will be eternal life; for the unsubmissive who refused to take truth for their guide and took depravity instead, there will be anger and fury. Pain and suffering will come to every human being who employs himself in evil – Jews first, but Greeks as well; renown, honour and peace will come to everyone who does good – Jews first, but Greeks as well. God has no favourites.

MEDITATION

Once Pilate had handed Jesus over to the chief priests and rulers of the people to do with him what they pleased, the drama was virtually ended. In the Garden of Gethsemane, some twelve hours earlier, Jesus had made his perfect self-oblation through the eternal Spirit to his heavenly Father, had offered complete obedience of will, even to death. Man's disobedience and rejection of the Son of God had been decisively declared in the trial scenes, the scourging, and the mockery. Jesus was as good as dead; now all that remained was to set the external seal upon the living sacrifice of Jesus.

The evangelists, therefore, do not give a great deal of space to an account of the way of the cross and the crucifixion. They have prepared their readers so well by the preceding scenes and discourses, that there is no need for them to do so. The way of the cross in particular, which has become the subject of a quite lengthy popular devotion, is described by Matthew in one verse, by Mark in two, and by John in half of a verse. We must realize, however, that the devotion we know as the Stations of the Cross includes the whole meaning of the Passion, and so extends its scope to all of the material we are meditating upon in all of the five sorrowful mysteries of the Rosary. For the moment we will confine our thoughts to what we find in those few verses of the four evangelists in which they describe the road from Pilate's Pavement to Golgotha.

Even in its reticence, the few words about the way of the cross fill in adequately the picture of our Lord's genuine humanity and the reality of his suffering. He has suffered an agony of anticipation and of spiritual torment in the garden; he has suffered excruciating physical pain by a scourging severe enough to kill a weaker man; he has been humiliated and derided; and now he is expected to make a last killing effort to walk up the hill to his death. He is like an athlete being spurred on to run and win a gruelling race when all his strength is already spent. But whereas an athlete would have been rested and had his limbs anointed and massaged in preparation, Jesus had been anointed with blows and massaged on every inch of his body with the sharp teeth of a loaded lash. And whereas an athlete could have looked hopefully beyond the race to rest and refreshment, Jesus could look forward only to being nailed down upon a cross. Having been punished by others, Jesus was now expected to punish himself by making an almost impossible effort to get himself up the hill to Calvary.

This episode makes very plain that our Lord's divinity never for a moment relieved him of any of the burden which as man he had to carry. It is to impress upon us that Jesus, in his human nature, and without any mitigation from his divine nature, bore all the weight of his cross and what it signified that St John says, 'carrying his own cross he went out of the city to the place of the skull'. The heavenly Father did not spare his only Son – not even when he was at his last gasp. And this implies no callousness on the Father's part, for he too was giving, giving his only Son for the sake of the world. The world could not be redeemed without this complete and unassisted sacrifice, and the Father was willing to see it carried out. 'God loved the world so much that he gave his only Son' (John 3.16). St John no doubt saw the completeness of our Lord's acceptance of the cross prefigured in the story of the sacrifice of Isaac. There, in Genesis chapter 22, we read that 'Abraham took the wood for the burnt offering, loaded it on Isaac, and carried in his own hands the fire and the knife'. The son Isaac had to carry the whole weight of the wood for the sacrificial fire, but Abraham must have felt the knife he carried piercing his own heart.

By stating that Jesus carried his own cross, St John is stressing the fact that Jesus was unassisted in his human nature by the privilege of his oneness with the Father. The cross symbolized the sin of all mankind, and that weight Jesus, the Son, had to bear entirely by himself. St John, in harmony with the overall method of his Gospel, is making a theological point; the other three evangelists are reporting external facts. Simon of Cyrene carried the cross, but did not in the least alleviate our Lord's sufferings. If he can be said to have assisted our Lord, he assisted him to fill up the cup of his agony by deferring his collapse and death until after he had suffered the final torture of the nails and cramps of crucifixion. Our Lord's executioners were being kind to be cruel. And if Simon did not lessen our Lord's physical suffering, still less can he be said to have assisted in carrying the cross in the sense in which St John uses that phrase. Nothing that any man can do can lift the least bit of weight of the sin of the world. Only Jesus Christ, Son of God and son of man, can do that.

The evangelist who devotes most space to the carrying of the cross is St Luke. His account runs to seven verses, and includes the report that women of Jerusalem showed compassion for our Lord as he passed by. This little touch is a reminder that although rejection of Jesus in some measure burdens every human conscience, rejection is not the final response to Jesus' revelation of the love of God. These women are a sign of a stirring of faith, love and hope; and Jesus, for his part, showed compassion for them, and urged them to pray for themselves, for there were to be dark days ahead. First he alluded to a prophecy of Hosea telling of how God would punish Israel for its idolatry, then to a prophecy of Ezekiel similarly telling of God's wrath upon Israel, and of how God would send a fire so terrible that it would devour growing green vegetation. How much worse, then, will it be for the dry brushwood that deserves to be burned up?

In this way, in the very moment of his death, our Lord

declared his trust in the perfect justice of his Father in heaven. The judgement he suffered would recoil upon the heads of his accusers, and upon all who remain impenitent and refuse to receive him as Lord. And yet, he did not invoke these warning prophecies as any kind of vengeful threat, but in a tone of solicitous appeal and of hope, as in the final stanza of Psalm 69:

> For God will save Zion,
> and rebuild the towns of Judah:
> they will be lived in, owned,
> handed down to his servants' descendants,
> and lived in by those who love his name.

THE WAY TO CALVARY: LUKE 23.26–32

As they were leading him away they seized on a man, Simon from Cyrene, who was coming in from the country, and made him shoulder the cross and carry it behind Jesus. Large numbers of people followed him, and of women too, who mourned and lamented for him. But Jesus turned to them and said, 'Daughters of Jerusalem, do not weep for me; weep rather for yourselves and for your children. For the days will surely come when people will say, "Happy are those who are barren, the wombs that have never borne, the breasts that have never suckled!" Then they will begin to say to the mountains, "Fall on us!"; to the hills, "Cover us!" For if men use the green wood like this, what will happen when it is dry?' Now with him they were also leading out two other criminals to be executed.

5

The Crucifixion

The Passover: Exodus 12.21–7

Moses summoned all the elders of Israel and said to them, 'Go and choose animals from the flock on behalf of your families, and kill the Passover victim. Then take a spray of hyssop, dip it in the blood that is in the basin, and with the blood from the basin touch the lintel and the two door-posts. Let none of you venture out of the house till morning. Then, when Yahweh goes through Egypt to strike it, and sees the blood on the lintel and on the two doorposts, he will pass over the door and not allow the destroyer to enter your homes and strike. You must keep these rules as an ordinance for all time for you and your children. When you enter the land that Yahweh is giving you, as he promised, you, must keep to this ritual. And when your children ask you, "What does this ritual mean?" you will tell them, "It is the sacrifice of the Passover in honour of Yahweh who passed over the houses of the sons of Israel in Egypt, and struck Egypt but spared our houses".' And the people bowed down and worshipped.

Christ sacrificed himself: Hebrews 9.24–8

It is not as though Christ had entered a man-made sanc-tuary which was only modelled on the real one; but it was heaven itself, so that he could appear in the actual pres-ence of God on our behalf. And he does not have to offer himself again and again, like the high priest going into the sanctuary year after year with the blood that is not his own, or else he would have had to suffer over and over again since the world began. Instead of that, he has made his appearance once and for all, now at the end of the last age, to do away with sin by sacrificing himself. Since men only die once, and after that comes judgement, so Christ, too, offers himself only once to take the faults of many on himself, and when he appears a second time, it will not be to deal with sin but to reward with salvation those who are waiting for him.

By his wounds we are healed: Isaiah 52.14–53.5
As the crowds were appalled on seeing him
– so disfigured did he look
that he seemed no longer human –
so will the crowds be astonished at him,
and kings stand speechless before him;
for they shall see something never told
and witness something never heard before:
'Who could believe what we have heard,
and to whom has the power of Yahweh been revealed?'
Like a sapling he grew up in front of us,
like a root in arid ground.
Without beauty, without majesty (we saw him),
no looks to attract our eyes;
a thing despised and rejected by men,
a man of sorrows and familiar with suffering,
a man to make people screen their faces;
he was despised and we took no account of him.

And yet ours were the sufferings he bore,
ours the sorrows he carried.
But we, we thought of him as someone punished,
struck by God, and brought low.
Yet he was pierced through for our faults,
crushed for our sins.
On him lies a punishment that brings us peace,
and through his wounds we are healed.

Scorn of mankind, jest of the people: Psalm 22.1–8
　　My God, my God, why have you deserted me?
　　How far from saving me, the words I groan!
　　I call all day, my God, but you never answer,
　　all night long I call and cannot rest.
　　Yet, Holy One, you
　　who make your home in the praises of Israel,
　　in you our fathers put their trust,
　　they trusted and you rescued them;
　　they called to you for help and they were saved,
　　they never trusted you in vain.

　　Yet here am I, now more worm than man,
　　scorn of mankind, jest of the people,
　　all who see me jeer at me,
　　they toss their heads and sneer,
　　'He relied on Yahweh, let Yahweh save him!
　　If Yahweh is his friend, let Him rescue him!

Mother of the redeemed: John 19.25–7
Near the cross of Jesus stood his mother and his mother's
sister, Mary the wife of Clopas, and Mary of Magdala.
Seeing his mother and the disciple he loved standing near
her, Jesus said to his mother, 'Woman, this is your son'.
Then to the disciple he said, 'This is your mother'. And
from that moment the disciple made a place for her in his
home.

MEDITATION

Having reached Golgotha, the place of a skull, Jesus' executioners brutally nailed him down through wrists and ankles to the cross, and then, pushing the cross erect and jolting it into position, left him to die slowly upon it; for our Lord's vicarious sufferings, great as they already had been, would not be complete until he had made the last supreme oblation of life itself.

Jesus had said to his disciples: 'A man can have no greater love than to lay down his life for his friends' (John 15.13). Applied to his own self-sacrifice, however, these words of Jesus have a much deeper meaning than appears on the surface, and the comment of one of the criminals crucified beside him gives the clue to that deeper meaning. The 'good thief' said to his companion: 'We got the same sentence as he did, but in our case we deserved it: we are paying for what we did. But this man has done nothing wrong'. The most important thing to meditate upon is not that Jesus died an untimely death, but simply that he died, for death is specifically the primeval curse upon sin, and Jesus was completely sinless; and as if that were not enough, the utter injustice of the condemnation is heightened by the form of his death, for the Jewish Law said: 'Cursed be everyone who is hanged upon a tree'. Thus behind the outward event of Jesus' death lies a mysterious happening: the payment of a debt by one who in no sense at all incurred that debt. This complete innocence of Jesus, allied to the divinity of his person, is what endows that payment with its perfect efficacy to cancel all sin and reconcile mankind with God.

All of the evangelists tell the story of the crucifixion so as to point clearly to this fact of atonement, of reconciliation between God and man through the sacrifice of Christ in man's place. The inclusion of the two criminals in the crucifixion group is the evangelists' way of recalling the fourth song of the servant of Yahweh (Isaiah 52.13–53.12) where the prophet speaks of this suffering servant 'letting himself be taken for a sinner'. It is that song too that declares:

> And yet ours were the sufferings he bore,
> ours the sorrows he carried.
> Yet he was pierced through for our faults,
> crushed for our sins.
> ...
> On him lies a punishment that brings us peace,
> and through his wounds we are healed.

The incongruous trio upon Calvary may also, in the inspired imagination of the evangelists, call to mind the mercy-seat of God within the Holy of Holies, the 'propitiatory', upon which, once a year, the high priest sprinkled the blood of a goat in atonement for the sins of Israel. This mercy-seat, symbol of God's presence, was flanked on each side by the figure of a cherub with wings upraised. In keeping with the inversion of values, which we have seen to characterize all of our Lord's passion, these angelic beings have been changed into two criminals, one on each side of the real presence of God upon the cross, a transformation which symbolizes the derision to which the Son of God was being subjected, as it also symbolizes, ironically, the real depths of God's mercy in stooping so close to sinful men.

The Temple itself, wherein so many propitiatory sacrifices took place, is explicitly mentioned early on in the crucifixion scene by those who jeered: 'So you would destroy the Temple and rebuild it in three days! Then save yourself: come down from the cross!' This unwitting testimony to what is about to happen in its completion in the Resurrection, reminds us that Jesus is the true Temple wherein alone real atonement is taking place.

The seamless robe of Christ, pointedly drawn to our attention when we see the soldiers casting lots for possession of it, is likewise a link with the Jewish ritual of atonement. The High Priest, whose duty it was once a year to enter the Holy of Holies and offer the propitiatory sacrifice, wore just such a robe as this.

The rending of the Temple veil, which occurred at the moment of our Lord's death, is even more significant, for it proclaims that Jesus is at that moment entering once and for all into the real Holy of Holies and making a real, not a symbolic, sacrifice of atonement. This thought is expounded at length in Hebrews chapters 7–9.

The atoning power of our Lord's death upon the cross is declared, above all perhaps, by the clear association of the crucifixion with the feast of the Passover. All of the events of the passion occurred at Passover time. St John in particular goes out of his way to synchronize exactly the time of the crucifixion with the time when, in the Temple close by, the priests were slaughtering the paschal lambs for yet another Passover festival. The blood of the paschal lamb, sprinkled on the lintel and door-posts of every Israelite house in Egypt at the first Passover, had caused the Lord to pass over these houses and spare the occupants. So now, the blood of Jesus, shed upon the crossbeam and upright post of the cross, enabled the Lord God at last to pass over all the sins of the new Israel, of those, that is, who believe in the Son of God, hanging upon the cross.

Not only the evangelists, but the other New Testament writers look back to the death of Jesus as the pivot of redemption, the unique atoning event, without which the forgiving power of God's love could not have achieved its effect upon mankind. St Peter very simply says: 'Christ suffered for you ... He had not done anything wrong ... He was bearing our faults in his own body on the cross, so that we might die to our faults and live for holiness; through his wounds you have been healed' (1 Pet. 2.21–4). St Paul writes:

'He has overridden the Law, and cancelled every record of the debt that we had to pay; he has done away with it by nailing it to the cross (Col. 2.14). And to the Corinthians he wrote: 'For our sake God made the sinless one into sin, so that in him we might become the goodness of God' (2 Cor. 5.21).

It is possible to think of the mystery of the atonement in a legalistic fashion, but such a concept is inadequate. Our reconciliation with God the Father through the passion and death of his Son did not result from the Father's being placated by the agonies of his Son. We ought rather to think of Christ's passion as the price he had to pay to accomplish the reparation of all the faults of mankind. Our Lord undid all the evil that mankind has wrought since the beginning of time, and made good all the deficit in good that men and women should have done for the glory of God. To achieve this it cost the Son of God unimaginable effort and pain and, in the end, his life. To think of the atonement as a kind of deal between God the Father and God the Son is to think far too negatively. Mankind has not been 'let off' because Christ suffered, but has been remade at the cost of Christ's agony and death. Knowing that this is so is what lifts the burden of guilt from our souls, for when we truly repent of our past sins and failures we desire above all to make up for all our faults; we cannot do this, but our Lord has done this for us. He was made 'sin for us', but has also become our righteousness.

Having wholeheartedly accepted this great gift we can then look forward to a life of virtue in the power of the Holy Spirit. The part we have to play is to be thankful and accept the responsibility that becomes ours because we now share in the Spirit of Christ.

The work of atonement is completed by the Holy Spirit working in us.

During the crucifixion (so three of the evangelists tell us) there was an eclipse of the sun. Matthew adds that as Jesus died the earth quaked and the tombs opened to give up the bodies of many holy men. These phenomena had been foretold by the prophets as signs of the day of the Lord. These signs impressed even the Roman soldiers, who declared: 'In truth this was a son of God.' The mention of the release of men already dead proclaims that Christ's atoning death was retrospectively effective for all of the faithful since the world began. St Peter corroborates this fact when he writes: 'in the spirit he went to preach to the spirits in prison' (I Pet. 3.19, cf. also I Pet. 4.5–6).

As he hung upon the cross Jesus uttered the opening lines of Psalm 22: 'My God, my God, why have you deserted me?' The mention of the vinegar, which someone offered him, draws our attention to Psalm 69 also. Both of these psalms indicate how real was our Lord's human dread and desolation at the prospect of death. Our Lord drained the cup of human suffering to the dregs with no mitigation by his divinity. We see our Lord's final sip of vinegar as a symbol of his draining the cup of bitterness to the dregs. If, however, we read these two psalms right through, we discover that both end in a note of triumph. Psalm 22 ends with these words:

> The whole earth, from end to end, will remember and
>   come back to Yahweh;
> all the families of the nations will bow down before him.
> For Yahweh reigns, the ruler of nations!
> Before him all the prosperous of the earth will bow
>   down,
> before him will bow all who go down to the dust.
> And my soul will live for him, my children will serve him;
> men will proclaim the Lord to generations still to come,
> his righteousness to a people yet unborn. All this he
>   has done.

All of the evangelists declare this triumph by the manner in which they describe the actual moment of our Lord's death. Matthew, Mark and Luke say that Jesus cried out in a loud voice and gave up his spirit. Luke tells us that he said: 'Father, into your hands I commend my spirit', one of the night prayers for Jewish children that his mother would have taught him. St John reports that he said: 'It is accomplished,' and adds that, 'bowing his head he gave up his spirit'. All of these descriptions affirm that there was something deliberate and positive about our Lord's dying. It was an act he performed, not a calamity he suffered. St John's phrase 'bowing his head' is significant, for once the head of a victim on a cross fell forward, breathing ceased almost immediately. His sufferings complete, and with the prospect now of merely struggling to enjoy a few minutes more of semiconscious life, Jesus submitted actively and willingly to death by bowing his head in trust and adoration before his Father in heaven, rather than letting it fall against his will. This description and the interpretation of it are in harmony with our Lord's saying recorded in John 10.17–18.

> The Father loves me,
> because I lay down my life
> in order to take it up again.
> No one takes it from me;
> I lay it down of my own free will.

Another important detail is the picture of Jesus breathing out his last breath. In this we have a hint of the new life of the Spirit emanating from him in his death and Resurrection, and passing on into his new people. This allusion to the new life of the Church is expressed more explicitly in two ways by St John. First he depicts Mary, the mother of Jesus, at the foot of the cross in company with the beloved disciple, who may well have been the evangelist himself. In the infancy story we learned that Mary was the perfect flowering of the Old Testament. She had learned all that the Lord had been teaching his ancient people of Israel. Through this perfection she had been counted worthy to bear the Son of God, the Saviour of the world. Now, as that Son is dying and in the act of opening the gates of new life to his new Israel, he declares that his own mother must also be the mother of that new people, represented by John, the beloved disciple. As he had been dependent upon her consent before he could assume the flesh which provided him with the means of redeeming mankind, so the Church, his many brethren, now turn to her, seeking help through her perpetual intercession.

The other mention of the Church to come is in the episode of the piercing of our Lord's side, when blood and water flowed out. This is a dramatic illustration of the fact that the Church, dependent for its life upon the sacraments of baptism and the Eucharist, is truly one in being with the very flesh and blood of Christ. There is a real flesh and blood connection, not just a moral connection, between Christ and his mystical body.

It is St Luke's Gospel we must thank for our knowledge of Christ's infancy, the narratives that supply the material of the Joyful Mysteries of the Rosary; it is most of all in St Luke's account of the passion that we find hints of joy and hope.

One of the thieves becomes contrite and is promised entry into paradise. The centurion ends up saying: 'This was a great and good man,' and the crowd go home 'beating their breasts'. Then Joseph of Arimathea, one of the Jewish leaders who had not consented to the condemnation of Jesus, appears and gives Jesus a costly burial (cf. John 19.39) in a tomb close by the place of execution ('They gave him a grave with the wicked, a tomb with the rich.' Isaiah 53.9). With a keen instinct for artistic unity, St Luke, having at the beginning of his narrative pictured Mary and Joseph wrapping the babe in swaddling clothes and laying him in a manger, rounds the story off with a picture of Joseph, another just man, having Jesus wrapped in a linen shroud and laying him in a tomb. In conclusion, St Luke makes a theological point too. He ends his account of our Lord's burial with the sentence: 'And on the Sabbath day they rested, as the Law required.' Not only did God's servants rest, but God himself, as after the six days of creation, now rested, for his work of re-creation was complete.

He suffered death and was buried: Luke 23.33–50

When they reached the place called The Skull,
they crucified him there and the two criminals
also, one on the right, the other on the left.
Jesus said, 'Father, forgive them; they do not
know what they are doing'. Then they cast lots
to share out his clothing.
The people stayed there watching him. As for
the leaders, they jeered at him. 'He saved
others,' they said 'let him save himself if he is
the Christ of God, the Chosen One.' The
soldiers mocked him too, and when they
approached to offer him vinegar they said, 'If
you are the king of the Jews, save yourself'.
Above him there was an inscription: 'This is the
King of the Jews'.
One of the criminals hanging there abused
him. 'Are you not the Christ?' he said. 'Save
yourself and us as well.' But the other spoke up
and rebuked him. 'Have you no fear of God at
all?' he said. 'You got the same sentence as he
did, but in our case we deserved it: we are
paying for what we did. But this man has done

nothing wrong. Jesus,' he said ' remember me when you come into your kingdom.' 'Indeed, I promise you,' he replied 'today you will be with me in paradise.'

It was now about the sixth hour and, with the sun eclipsed, a darkness came over the whole land until the ninth hour. The veil of the Temple was torn right down the middle; and when Jesus had cried out in a loud voice, he said, 'Father, into your hands I commit my spirit'. With these words he breathed his last. When the centurion saw what had taken place, he gave praise to God and said, 'This was a great and good man'. And when all the people who had gathered for the spectacle saw what had happened, they went home beating their breasts.

All his friends stood at a distance; so also did the women who had accompanied him from Galilee, and they saw all this happen.

Then a member of the council arrived, an upright and virtuous man named Joseph. He had not consented to what the others had planned and carried out. He came from Arimathaea, a Jewish town, and he lived in the hope of seeing the kingdom of God. This man went to Pilate and asked for the body of Jesus. He then took it down, wrapped it in a shroud and put him in a tomb which was hewn in stone in which no one had yet been laid. It was Preparation Day and the sabbath was imminent.

*Meanwhile the women who had come from
Galilee with Jesus were following behind. They
took note of the tomb and of the position of the
body.*
*Then they returned and prepared spices and
ointments. And on the sabbath day they rested,
as the Law required.*

PART FOUR

The Glorious
Mysteries

1

The Resurrection

The Garden of Life: Genesis 2.5–15

At the time when Yahweh God made earth and heaven there was as yet no wild bush on the earth nor had any wild plant yet sprung up, for Yahweh God had not sent rain on the earth, nor was there any man to till the soil. However, a flood was rising from the earth and watering all the surface of the soil. Yahweh God fashioned man of dust from the soil. Then he breathed into his nostrils a breath of life, and thus man became a living being.

Yahweh God planted a garden in Eden which is in the east, and there he put the man he had fashioned. Yahweh God caused to spring up from the soil every kind of tree, enticing to look at and good to eat, with the tree of life and the tree of the knowledge of good and evil in the middle of the garden. A river flowed from Eden to water the garden, and from there it divided to make four streams. The first is named the Pishon, and this encircles the whole land of Havilah where there is gold. The gold of this land is pure; bdellium and onyx stone are found there. The second river is named the Gihon, and this encircles the whole land of Cush. The third river is named the Tigris, and this flows to the east of Ashur. The fourth river is the Euphrates. Yahweh God took the man and settled him in the garden of Eden to cultivate and take care of it.

The empty tomb: John 20.1–10
It was very early on the first day of the week and still dark, when Mary of Magdala came to the tomb. She saw that the stone had been moved away from the tomb and came running to Simon Peter and the other disciple, the one Jesus loved. 'They have taken the Lord out of the tomb' she said 'and we don't know where they have put him.'

So Peter set out with the other disciple to go to the tomb. They ran together, but the other disciple, running faster than Peter, reached the tomb first; he bent down and saw the linen cloths lying on the ground, but did not go in. Simon Peter who was following now came up, went right into the tomb, saw the linen cloths on the ground, and also the cloth that had been over his head; this was not with the linen cloths but rolled up in a place by itself. Then the other disciple who had reached the tomb first also went in; he saw and he believed. Till this moment they had failed to understand the teaching of scripture, that he must rise from the dead. The disciples then went home again.

Believing is more than seeing: Luke 16.19–31
'There was a rich man who used to dress in purple and fine linen and feast magnificently every day. And at his gate there lay a poor man called Lazarus, covered with sores, who longed to fill himself with the scraps that fell from the rich man's table. Dogs even came and licked his sores. Now the poor man died and was carried away by the angels to the bosom of Abraham. The rich man also died and was buried.

'In his torment in Hades he looked up and saw Abraham a long way off with Lazarus in his bosom. So he cried out, "Father Abraham, pity me and send Lazarus to dip the tip of his finger in water and cool my tongue, for I am in agony in these flames". "My son," Abraham replied "remember that during your life good things came your way, just as bad things came the way of Lazarus. Now he is being comforted here while you are in

agony. But that is not all: between us and you a great gulf
has been fixed, to stop anyone, if he wanted to, crossing
from our side to yours, and to stop any crossing from
your side to ours."

'The rich man replied, "Father, I beg you then to send
Lazarus to my father's house, since I have five brothers, to
give them warning so that they do not come to this place
of torment too". "They have Moses and the prophets,"
said Abraham "let them listen to them." Ah no, father
Abraham," said the rich man "but if someone comes to
them from the dead, they will repent." Then Abraham
said to him, "If they will not listen to either Moses or to
the prophets, they will not be convinced even if someone
should rise from the dead".'

My Lord and my God!: John 20.24–9
Thomas, called the Twin, who was one of the Twelve, was
not with them when Jesus came. When the disciples said,
'We have seen the Lord', he answered, 'Unless I see the
holes that the nails made in his hands and can put my
finger into the holes they made, and unless I can put my
hand into his side, I refuse to believe'. Eight days later the
disciples were in the house again and Thomas was with
them. The doors were closed, but Jesus came in and stood
among them. 'Peace be with you' he said. Then he spoke
to Thomas, 'Put your finger here; look, here are my
hands. Give me your hand; put it into my side. Doubt no
longer but believe.' Thomas replied, 'My Lord and my
God!' Jesus said to him:

'You believe because you can see me.
Happy are those who have not seen and yet believe.'

The Garden of Eternal Life: John 19.41–2 and John 20.11–18
At the place where he had been crucified there was a
garden, and in this garden a new tomb in which no one had
yet been buried. Since it was the Jewish Day of Preparation
and the tomb was near at hand, they laid Jesus there .

Meanwhile Mary stayed outside near the tomb, weeping. Then, still weeping, she stooped to look inside, and saw two angels in white sitting where the body of Jesus had been, one at the head, the other at the feet. They said, 'Woman, why are you weeping?' 'They have taken my Lord away' she replied 'and I don't know where they have put him.' As she said this she turned round and saw Jesus standing there, though she did not recognise him. Jesus said, 'Woman, why are you weeping? Who are you looking for?' Supposing him to be the gardener, she said, 'Sir, if you have taken him away, tell me where you have put him, and I will go and remove him'. Jesus said. 'Mary!' She knew him then and said to him in Hebrew, 'Rabbuni' – which means Master. Jesus said to her, 'Do not cling to me, because I have not yet ascended to the Father. But go and find the brothers, and tell them: I am ascending to my Father and your Father, to my God and your God.' So Mary of Magdala went and told the disciples that she had seen the Lord and that he had said these things to her.

MEDITATION

All through his Gospel, St John looks forward to our Lord's being raised up on the cross, which he sees as his glorification. Jesus had said: 'The Son of Man must be lifted up ... so that everyone who believes may have eternal life in him' (John 3.13–15); and 'When you have lifted up the Son of Man, then you will know that I am He' (John 8.28); and 'When I am lifted up from the earth, I shall draw all men to myself' (John 12.32). On the eve of his death Jesus began his great priestly prayer with the words: 'Father, the hour has come: glorify your Son so that your Son may glorify you' (John 17.1). These sayings point to the Crucifixion as the triumphant climax of our Lord's work, the point where the Father would be supremely glorified in the Son. Consistent with this thought is John's emphasis upon our Lord's final cry from the cross: 'It is accomplished' (John 19.30).

The power of the Resurrection was latent in the triumph of the cross; but the disciples did not yet understand what was going on, even though our Lord had foretold what would happen to him. For them Jesus was simply dead and buried; the victory of the cross still had to be revealed to them. The record of that revelation, and comment on what precisely that revelation meant, are contained in the concluding chapters of the four Gospels.

The Sabbath rest over, some women went to the tomb with spices, expecting to find the corpse of Jesus. To their amazement they found the stone rolled away and the tomb empty. Thereupon two angels appeared to them and told them that Jesus had risen from the dead. The women returned and told the apostles what they had seen and heard, but the apostles regarded their story as 'pure nonsense' (Luke 24.11). St Luke reports: 'Peter, however, went running to the tomb. He bent down and saw the binding cloths but nothing else; he then went back home, amazed at what had happened.' This amazement does not seem to have amounted to understanding or belief. Later in the same day the Lord appeared to two disciples on the road to Emmaus, but they did not recognize him. He said to them: 'You foolish men! So slow to believe the full message of the prophets!' On the evening of the same day, when Jesus appeared to the assembled company of apostles, these too did not immediately believe it was he, but thought they were seeing a ghost.

These records in the Gospels teach us that to believe in the risen Lord is not a matter simply of physical sight. Seeing is not necessarily believing. The parable of the rich man and the beggar (Luke 16.19–31) is about this very problem. The rich man asks that the beggar be sent back from the dead to warn his brothers to mend their ways. He is told: 'They have Moses and the prophets, let them listen to them. If they will not listen either to Moses or to the prophets, they will not be convinced even if someone should rise from the dead.' That is why our Lord had to elicit the faith of the two disciples on the road to Emmaus, and of the company of apostles, by expounding for them the meaning of the Scriptures (Luke 24.25–7; 44–6), for no miracle, not even his own rising from the dead can convince any man unless, through diligent attention to the word of God, declared principally in the Scriptures, he has acquired the disposition that is able to blossom into full faith in Jesus as Lord. This predisposition towards the fullness of faith can be found in any who, in the words of the Vatican Council II document *Lumen Gentium*, n.16, 'seek God with a sincere heart and, moved by grace, try in their actions to do his will as they know it through the dictates of their conscience.'

For us who live two thousand years after the Resurrection that is comforting. It means that we are no less, and no more, capable of finding true faith in our risen Lord than were those who saw him with their own eyes. The power to believe comes from an inner understanding of the meaning of our Lord's death and Resurrection. This understanding, this faith, is something we must pray for, because, as our Lord said: 'No one can come to me unless he is drawn by the Father who sent me' (John 6.44).

St John tells us that Peter was accompanied to the tomb by 'the other disciple, the one Jesus loved', and that this disciple – almost certainly John himself – going in after Peter, 'saw and believed'. This, then, is the record of the first act of true belief in the risen Lord – and it took place on the evidence of the empty tomb, not on the evidence of sight of the risen Lord. What was it that John believed? Not simply that Jesus had been resuscitated, as Lazarus had been, so that he could enjoy a few more years in the company of his friends, but that he was truly what he had claimed to be: the incarnate Son of God, now risen from the dead and living for ever in the light of heaven.

St John's report of our Lord's appearance to Mary Magdalene very early in the morning – just after his own act of belief – makes the same statement. At first she did not recognize him, but after he had addressed her by name she responded with the cry, 'Rabbuni!' This form of address, more solemn than 'Rabbi', was often used when addressing God; it is her profession of faith in the risen Jesus as the Son of God.

St John concludes the main part of his Gospel with a report of our Lord's appearance after a week to St Thomas who had previously doubted the testimony of the other apostles. Thomas' final response is the same: 'My Lord and my God'. Faith is fundamentally belief that Jesus is truly God's own Son, crucified and now risen from the dead to enjoy eternal glory with the Father; and this faith in Christ is joined with complete subjection to him of mind, heart and will. Jesus' reply to Thomas's declaration of faith underlines what we noted already, that faith can come equally to men of all times in response to the testimony of the apostles, and is not dependent upon physical sight.

St John concludes this account by saying that it was to invite others in all ages to share this life-giving faith that he has recorded a selection of the 'signs that Jesus worked'. 'These are recorded so that you may believe that Jesus is the Christ, the Son of God, and that believing this you may have life through his name' (John 20.31).

In these concluding words St John declares the purpose behind all the mysterious events that have culminated in the glory of Christ's Resurrection: that believers may share in this new life of the risen Lord. It is no accident, therefore, that our Lord appeared to Mary Magdalene in a garden, and sent her with a message to 'the brothers', the only time, according to St John, that Jesus used that word of his disciples. Our Lord's victory over death was not a private reward but a victory to be shared with all his brothers; and that gift consisted in taking them back to the state of innocence which man had enjoyed in the garden of Eden. Our Lord's atoning sacrifice is seen from the perspective of the Resurrection as no legal fiction, but as a real reinstatement of mankind in its primeval state. This is the foundation of the new life in the Spirit, of which St Paul has so much to say in his letters, and about which we must continue to meditate as we turn our thoughts to Christ's return to heavenly glory.

ON THE THIRD DAY HE ROSE AGAIN:
LUKE 24.1–8

On the first day of the week, at the first sign of dawn, they went to the tomb with the spices they had prepared. The found that the stone had been rolled away from the tomb, but on entering discovered that the body of the Lord Jesus was not there. As they stood there not knowing what to think, two men in brilliant clothes suddenly appeared at their side. Terrified, the women lowered their eyes. But the two men said to them, 'Why look among the dead for someone who is alive? He is not here; he has risen. Remember what he told you when he was still in Galilee: that the Son of Man had to be handed over into the power of sinful men and be crucified, and rise again on the third day.' And they remembered his words.

2

The Ascension

Elijah is assumed into heaven 2 Kings 2.5–13

The brotherhood of prophets who live at Jericho went up to Elisha and said, 'Do you know that Yahweh is going to carry your lord and master away today?' 'Yes, I know,' he said 'be quiet.' Elijah said, 'Elisha, please stay here, Yahweh is only sending me to the Jordan'. But he replied, 'As Yahweh lives and as you yourself live, I will not leave you!' And they went on together.

Fifty of the brotherhood of prophets followed them, halting some distance away as the two of them stood beside the Jordan. Elijah took his cloak, rolled it up and struck the water; and the water divided to left and right, and the two of them crossed over dry-shod. When they had crossed, Elijah said to Elisha. 'Make your request. What can I do for you before I am taken from you?' Elisha answered, 'Let me inherit a double share of your spirit'. 'Your request is a difficult one' Elijah said. 'If you see me while I am being taken from you, it shall be as you ask; if not, it will not be so.' Now as they walked on, talking as they went, a chariot of fire appeared and horses of fire, coming between the two of them; and Elijah went up to heaven in the whirlwind. Elisha saw it, and shouted, 'My father! My father! Chariot of Israel and its chargers!' Then he lost sight of him, and taking hold of his clothes he tore them in half. He picked up the cloak of Elijah which had fallen, and went back and stood on the bank of the Jordan.

Gone to take his place: Hebrews 1.1–4

At various times in the past and in various different ways, God spoke to our ancestors through the prophets; but in our own time, the last days, he has spoken to us through his Son, the Son that he has appointed to inherit everything and through whom he made everything there is. He is the radiant light of God's glory and the perfect copy of his nature, sustaining the universe by his powerful command; and now that he has destroyed the defilement of sin, he has gone to take his place in heaven at the right hand of divine Majesty. So he is now as far above the angels as the title which he has inherited is higher than their own name.

The Faith in a nutshell: 1 Timothy 3.16
He was made visible in the flesh,
attested by the Spirit,
seen by angels,
proclaimed to the pagans,
believed in by the world,
taken up in glory.

The Judgement: John 5.21–4
Thus, as the Father raises the dead and gives them life,
so the Son gives life to anyone he chooses;
for the Father judges no one;
he has entrusted all judgement to the Son,
so that all may honour the Son
as they honour the Father.
Whoever refuses honour to the Son
refuses honour to the Father who sent him.
I tell you most solemnly,
whoever listens to my words,
and believes in the one who sent me,
has eternal life;
without being brought to judgement
he has passed from death to life.

A heavenly mind: Colossians 3.1–4

Since you have been brought back to true life with Christ, you must look for the things that are in heaven, where Christ is, sitting at God's right hand. Let your thoughts be on heavenly things, not on the things that are on the earth, because you have died, and now the life you have is hidden with Christ in God. But when Christ is revealed – and he is your life – you too will be revealed in all your glory with him.

MEDITATION

The temptation to 'freeze' separate scenes in the story of man's redemption is nowhere more sedulously to be resisted than in respect of the Mysteries of the Rosary entitled Crucifixion, Resurrection and Ascension. All three together make up the revelation of God's glory in his Son, and of the mystery of eternal life shed into the hearts of men. With the Crucifixion we associate principally the atonement, the making up for the sins of all mankind. St Paul writes: 'God dealt with sin by sending his own Son in a body as physical as any sinful body, and in that body God condemned sin. He did this in order that the Law's just demands might be satisfied in us' (Romans 8.3–4). With the Resurrection we associate principally the victory of Christ's sacrificial death, his own restoration to life, and the prospect of our sharing in the sinless life that such mankind was intended to possess. 'If the Spirit of him who raised Jesus from the dead is living in you, then he who raised Jesus from the dead will give life to your own mortal bodies through his Spirit living in you' (Romans 8.11). With the Ascension we associate principally our looking ahead to the time when heaven and earth pass away and Christ comes again to judge mankind, and when we, the process of our sanctification complete, will come to share in Christ's glory in heaven. 'Blessed be God the Father of our Lord Jesus Christ, who in his great mercy has given us a new birth as his sons, by raising Jesus Christ from the dead, so that we have a sure hope and the promise of an inheritance that can never be spoilt or soiled and never fade away, because it is being kept for you in the heavens' (1 Peter 1.3–4).

The Ascension, the final farewell of the Lord to the world of time and space, was the logical conclusion to his glorification through death and Resurrection. His presence with the disciples in their visible and tangible world was clearly a temporary episode, sufficient to complete the revelation to men of the mystery of the Word made flesh. The evangelists do not, therefore, spend much time describing the episode. St Matthew merely records our Lord's final commission to the apostles: 'Go, therefore, make disciples of all the nations; baptise them in the name of the Father and of the Son and of the Holy Spirit, and teach them to observe all the commands I gave you. And know that I am with you always; yes, to the end of time' (Matthew 28.19–20), but does not mention his departure. Mark ends his story similarly with the commissioning of the apostles, but adds that the Lord 'was taken up into heaven'. Luke records the command to wait in Jerusalem until they had received power from on high, and then briefly describes how Jesus blessed them and 'was carried up to heaven'. St John is silent about the Ascension: he has already told us sufficient to make the Ascension an inevitable conclusion we can draw for ourselves. In the Acts of the Apostles St Luke repeats his account of the Ascension, ending with the comment of two angels: 'Why are you men from Galilee standing here looking into the sky? Jesus who has been taken up from you into heaven, this same Jesus will come back in the same way as you have seen him go there', as though saying, 'He is gone for good; it is up to you to get on with the job of preaching his gospel throughout the world, and getting yourselves ready for the day of judgement, when you will see him again'.

Meditation on the Ascension ends up, therefore, not in dreamy stargazing, but in practical consideration of how the life of the Spirit really works out in our lives here on earth. And that is quite simply because the life of the Spirit – the life of heaven, that is – is not something that will begin in the hereafter, but something that begins the moment we are baptized, and goes on until it merges into the timeless life of heaven. St John reports our Lord's saying:

Whoever listens to my words,
and believes in the one who sent me,
has eternal life;

...

the hour will come – in fact, it is here already –
when the dead will hear the voice of the Son of God,
and all who hear it will live. (John 5.24–5)

St Paul, too, links Christ's Resurrection with the life we live while still on this earth. 'If the Spirit of him who raised Jesus from the dead is living in you, then he who raised Jesus from the dead will give life to your own mortal bodies through his Spirit living in you' (Romans 8.11).

St Paul, whose letters make up roughly one quarter of the New Testament, is writing nearly all the time about the reality of the life we now live by the power of the Holy Spirit, a life that begins in the innocence conferred through faith and baptism and proceeds, through many struggles and setbacks, towards one goal: perfection – the perfection that we hope to be able to present before our Lord when he comes to be our judge. But St Paul's teaching is anything but a type of dreary moralizing. The point from which he starts is that morality – striving to keep the Law by our own unaided efforts – has miserably failed and always will fail, because man in his natural state is powerless to please God by keeping the Law, so that the Law in the end can only condemn him, although the Law itself is 'sacred, and what it commands is sacred, just and good' (Romans 7.12). At the heart of St Paul's insistent and repeated exhortations to seek perfection: 'Be like children of light, for the effects of the light are seen in complete goodness and right living and truth' (Eph. 5.8–9), is the declaration that the new life from which such perfect goodness flows comes as a free gift from God, appropriated only through faith and baptism. 'It is by faith and through Jesus that we have entered this state of grace' (Romans 5.2). Faith and baptism are the link between the believer and the purifying power of Christ's sacrifice, that 'union with Christ' by which we 'have imitated his death' (Romans 6.5). Into the soul thus purified God is able to pour the life of the Spirit, so that the Christian can say, 'I have been crucified with Christ, and I live now not with my own life but with the life of Christ who lives in me.' (Galations 2.19–20).

St Paul thus resolves any tension there might seem to be between faith and good works. He stresses on the one hand that atonement is the work of Christ alone, and that we benefit from that atonement purely by God's free gift, grasped through faith. On the other hand he insists that this justification by faith is a re-creation of our being, which must issue in a life of moral perfection, a life that must always be acknowledged as the life of Christ in us. 'When we were baptised we went into the tomb with him and joined him in death, so that as Christ was raised from the dead by the Father's glory, we too might live a new life' (Romans 6.4). Our mystical union with Christ, crucified, risen, and ascended, is the foundation of the Good News St Paul preached. It is a message of life: 'Let your thoughts be on heavenly things, not on the things that are on the earth, because you have died, and now the life you have is hidden with Christ in God. But when Christ is revealed – and he is your life – you too will be revealed in all your glory with him' (Colossians 3.2–4).

HE BLESSED THEM AND WAS CARRIED UP TO HEAVEN: LUKE 24.44–8, 50–3

Then he told them, 'This is what meant when I said, while I was still with you, that everything written about me in the Law of Moses, in the Prophets and in the Psalms, has to be fulfilled'. He then opened their minds to understand the scriptures, and he said to them, 'So you see how it is written that the Christ would suffer and on the third day rise from the dead, and that, in his name, repentance for the forgiveness of sins would be preached to all the nations, beginning from Jerusalem. You are witnesses to this.

Then he took them out as far as the outskirts of Bethany, and lifting up his hands he blessed them. Now as he blessed them, he withdrew from them and was carried up to heaven. They worshipped him and then went back to Jerusalem full of joy; and they were continually in the Temple praising God.

3

The Descent of the Holy Spirit

The Spirit of love: Romans 5.1–5
So far then we have seen that, through our Lord Jesus Christ, by faith we are judged righteous and at peace with God, since it is by faith and through Jesus that we have entered this state of grace in which we can boast about looking forward to God's glory. But that is not all we can boast about; we can boast about our sufferings. These sufferings bring patience, as we know, and patience brings perseverance, and perseverance brings hope, and this hope is not deceptive, because the love of God has been poured into our hearts by the Holy Spirit which has been given us.

The Spirit of unity: 1 Corinthians 12.4–11
There is a variety of gifts but always the same Spirit; there are all sorts of service to be done, but always to the same Lord; working in all sorts of different ways in different people, it is the same God who is working in all of them. The particular way in which the Spirit is given to each person is for a good purpose. One may have the gift of preaching with wisdom given him by the Spirit; another may have the gift of preaching instruction given him by the same Spirit; and another again the gift of faith given by the same Spirit; another the gift of healing, through

this one Spirit; one the power of miracles; another, prophecy; another the gift of recognising spirits; another the gift of tongues and another the ability to interpret them. All these are the work of one and the same Spirit, who distributes different gifts to different people just as he chooses.

The old covenant: Exodus 24.12–18

Yahweh said to Moses, 'Come up to me on the mountain and stay there while I give you the stone tablets – the law and the commandments – that I have written for their instruction'. Accordingly Moses rose, he and his servant Joshua, and they went up the mountain of God. To the elders he had said, 'Wait here for us until we come back to you. You have Aaron and Hur with you; if anyone has a difference to settle, let him go to them.' And Moses went up the mountain.

The cloud covered the mountain, and the glory of Yahweh settled on the mountain of Sinai; for six days the cloud covered it, and on the seventh day Yahweh called to Moses from inside the cloud. To the eyes of the sons of Israel the glory of Yahweh seemed like a devouring fire on the mountain top. Moses went right into the cloud. He went up the mountain, and stayed there for forty days and forty nights.

Discord over all the earth: Genesis 11.1–9

Throughout the earth men spoke the same language, with the same vocabulary. Now as they moved eastwards they found a plain in the land of Shinar where they settled. They said to one another, 'Come, let us make bricks and bake them in the fire'. – For stone they used bricks, and for mortar they used bitumen. – 'Come,' they said 'let us build ourselves a town and a tower with its top reaching heaven. Let us make a name for ourselves, so that we may not be scattered about the whole earth.'

Now Yahweh came down to see the town and the tower that the sons of man had built. 'So they are all a single people with a single language!' said Yahweh. 'This is but the start of their undertakings! There will be nothing too hard for them to do. Come, let us go down and confuse their language on the spot so that they can no longer understand one another.' Yahweh scattered them thence over the whole face of the earth, and they stopped building the town. It was named Babel therefore, because there Yahweh confused the language of the whole earth. It was from there that Yahweh scattered them over the whole face of the earth.

Harmony restored to mankind: Acts 2.1–9
When Pentecost day came round, they had all met in one room, when suddenly they heard what sounded like a powerful wind from heaven, the noise of which filled the entire house in which they were sitting; and something appeared to them that seemed like tongues of fire; these separated and came to rest on the head of each of them. They were all filled with the Holy Spirit, and began to speak foreign languages as the Spirit gave them the gift of speech.

Now there were devout men living in Jerusalem from every nation under heaven, and at this sound they all assembled, each one bewildered to hear these men speaking his own language. They were amazed and astonished. 'Surely' they said 'all these men speaking are Galileans? How does it happen that each of us hears them in his own native language? Parthians, Medes and Elamites; people from Mesopotamia, Judaea and Cappadocia, Pontus and Asia, Phrygia and Pamphylia, Egypt and the parts of Libya round Cyrene; as well as visitors from Rome – Jews and proselytes alike – Cretans and Arabs; we hear them preaching in our own language about the marvels of God.' Everyone was amazed and unable to explain it; they asked one another what it all meant. Some, however, laughed it off. 'They have been drinking too much new wine' they said.

MEDITATION

In the first three Mysteries of the Rosary the ancient people of God figure prominently in the scheme of salvation. This people and their history were God's word to mankind, and the preparation for the Incarnation of God's Son, the Word made flesh. The last three Joyful Mysteries again focus attention on the people of God, who have now become partners in a new covenant, a new relationship with Almighty God. The old relationship was valid while it lasted, but after the Word of God became flesh that relationship was transcended. No longer do the people of the covenant regard the law of God merely as a moral code that stands over against them, inscribed upon stone tablets, but as the mind of God living in their hearts through the indwelling of his Holy Spirit; no longer do the people of the covenant worship God merely in his symbolic presence in the Holy of Holies within the Temple, but in his real presence in the Holy Eucharist. The mystery of the Lord's presence, of his being Immanuel, God with us, extends further in that he is present in the people of the new covenant, through the gift of the Holy Spirit. Christ the Head, united with all his members, is the new temple of God, that will endure upon earth until the end of time. St Peter wrote to the early Christians: 'Set yourselves close to him so that you too, the holy priesthood that offers the spiritual sacrifices which Jesus Christ has made acceptable to God, may be living stones making a spiritual house' (I Peter 2.5).

It is the indwelling of the Holy Spirit which brings about the mystical union between the believer and Christ, and makes Christ's redemptive acts effective in the members of his body.

The account of the mystery of the indwelling of the Holy Spirit in the Church begins not with the Pentecost narrative in Acts, but with accounts in the Gospels that tell us of this mystery.

When dying on the cross, Jesus cried out with a loud voice 'and gave up his spirit'. Does this mean only that he died, or is it a hint that he was passing on his Spirit to others? St John tells us that on the very first Easter evening, immediately after greeting the apostles with the words: 'As the Father sent me, so I am sending you', Jesus breathed on them and said: 'Receive the Holy Spirit'. In this way St John links the giving of the Holy Spirit with the death and Resurrection of Jesus.

In his account of Christ's passion and death St John had already indicated this link. When the soldier pierced our Lord's side blood and water flowed from it. Early Christian writers saw this as a declaration that the Church was born from the side of Christ on the cross. The Holy Spirit was poured out then in the sacraments of the Eucharist and baptism. The Church is flesh of Christ's flesh and bone of his bone – truly his mystical body. Mystical union with Christ is membership in his mystical body; the new life of the Spirit begins in the individual at the moment of his baptism, and increases in strength by feeding on the substance of the risen Jesus Christ, true God and true man, under the sacramental signs of the Eucharist.

If the message of the birth of the Church through the gift of the Holy Spirit is told substantially in the context of the Resurrection; if, indeed, the Church can be said to have issued from the side of Christ upon the cross, just as Genesis tells us that Eve was made from Adam's rib while he slept, why the additional dramatic story of the outpouring of the Holy Spirit upon the Church at Pentecost, seven weeks after the Resurrection?

On the day of Pentecost the Church, already born from the side of Christ on the cross, came of age and was equipped with power to carry out in all the world the commission given her by Christ. At last, having waited for the appropriate length of time, the Church was now able to fulfil the commission given to her on the first Easter evening: 'As the Father sent me, so I am sending you.' On the day of Pentecost this enabling was manifested in the descent of the Holy Spirit upon the apostles, to the dramatic accompaniment of sights and sounds.

The fact that this public manifestation took place at Pentecost, the Jewish feast of Weeks, is significant, for just as the birth of the Church is linked with the Passover, so the coming of age of the Church is linked with the feast which celebrated both the wheat harvest and the giving of the Law to Moses on Sinai. There is a parallel between the New Testament account of Pentecost and the account of Moses on Mount Sinai. Before going up the mountain, Moses said to the elders of the people: 'Wait here for us until we come back to you' (Exodus 24.14); then he went up to meet God on Sinai, returning forty days later bringing the tablets of the Law with him. So in the New Testament, before ascending to his Father, Jesus said to the apostles: 'Stay in the city then, until you are clothed with the power from on high' (Luke 24.49); then on the day of Pentecost, the festival of the giving of the Law, he returned to his people in the power of the Holy Spirit. The details of the narrative and St Luke's manner of telling it teach us that the outpouring of the Spirit on the day of Pentecost was the ratifying of the new covenant with the new people of God, and their being commissioned to set out upon their pilgrimage of bearing witness to the love of God.

In the New Testament the Holy Spirit is spoken of as the Spirit of love, and love is the chief mark of the disciples of Christ. The New Testament emphasis on love is connected with the idea of the new covenant made at Pentecost with the new Israel. The prophet Jeremiah had proclaimed: 'The days are coming – it is Yahweh who speaks – when I will make a new covenant with the House of Israel ... Deep within them I will plant my Law'. The Law of God under the new covenant is no longer to be regarded as an external constraint, but as the mind and heart of God in which his people share, because they possess his Spirit. Love of God's commandments flows from this communion with God, made possible by Christ's gift of his Spirit; and love of one's neighbour, inseparable from love of God, is itself an immediate product of the love of God, which consists in perfect and joyful obedience to his commandments:

> We can be sure that we love God's children
> if we love God himself and do what he has commanded
>   us. (1 John 5.2)

The other great sign of the Spirit is unity. In the story of the Tower of Babel, the disharmony amongst men and women is symbolized and punished by the multiplication of languages, so that they can no longer communicate properly with each other. On the day of Pentecost the gift of languages is seen as a means of unifying the people. Now they can all understand the gospel and each other.

The book of Acts describes the Church as a united family, full of mutual respect, its structure firmly held together by the special functions conferred by the Spirit upon different members. St Paul too lays great stress upon the attribute of unity, and in 1 Corinthians 12.27–8 he lists a number of the different offices created in the Church by the Holy Spirit. Prominent among these are apostles, prophets and teachers. These various gifts or functions are permanent features of the visible Church, all truly spiritual in origin, and all necessary for the perfecting of God's purposes. All these gifts are manifestations, not of purely human qualities or power, but of love, which has its origin in Christ himself, from whom the Spirit flows. 'If we live by the truth and in love, we shall grow in all ways into Christ, who is the head by whom the whole body is fitted and joined together, every joint adding its own strength, for each separate part to work according to its function. So the body grows until it has built itself up, in love' (Ephesians 4.15–16).

'RECEIVE THE HOLY SPIRIT':
JOHN 20.19–23

*In the evening of that same day, the first day of
the week, the doors were closed in the room
where the disciples were, for fear of the Jews.
Jesus came and stood among them. He said to
them, 'Peace be with you', and showed them his
hands and his side. The disciples were filled
with joy when they saw the Lord, and he said to
them again, 'Peace be with you.*

*As the Father sent me,
so am I sending you.'*

After saying this he breathed on them and said:

*'Receive the Holy Spirit.
For those whose sins you forgive,
they are forgiven;
for those whose sins you retain,
they are retained.'*

4

The Assumption

Mother of the living: Genesis 3.14–16
Then the Lord God said to the serpent, 'Because you
have done this,

> 'Be accursed beyond all cattle,
> all wild beasts.
> You shall crawl on your belly and eat dust
> every day of your life.
> I will make you enemies of each other:
> you and the woman,
> your offspring and her offspring.
> It will crush your head
> and you will strike its heel.'

To the woman he said:

> 'I will multiply your pains in childbearing,
> you shall give birth to your children in pain.
> Your yearning shall be for your husband,
> yet he will lord it over you.'

My dove is unique: The Song of Songs 6.4–6, 9–10
> You are beautiful as Tirzah, my love,
> fair as Jerusalem.
> Turn your eyes away,
> for they hold me captive.
> Your hair is like a flock of goats
> frisking down the slopes of Gilead.

Your teeth are like a flock of sheep
as they come up from the washing.
...
But my dove is unique,
mine, unique and perfect.
She is the darling of her mother,
the favourite of the one who bore her.
The maidens saw her, and proclaimed her blessed,
queens and concubines sang her praises:
'Who is this arising like the dawn,
fair as the moon,
resplendent as the sun,
terrible as an army with banners?'

Obedience to the word: Luke 8.4–8, 19–21
With a large crowd gathering and people from every
town finding their way to him, he used this parable:
'A sower went out to sow his seed. As he sowed, some
fell on the edge of the path and was trampled on; and the
birds of the air ate it up. Some seed fell on rock, and when
it came up it withered away, having no moisture. Some
seed fell amongst thorns and the thorns grew with it and
choked it. And some seed fell into rich soil and grew and
produced its crop a hundredfold.' Saying this he cried, '
Listen, anyone who has ears to hear!'
...
His mother and his brothers came looking for him, but
they could not get to him because of the crowd. He was
told, 'Your mother and brothers are standing outside and
want to see you'. But he said in answer, 'My mother and
my brothers are those who hear the word of God and put
it into practice'.

On eagle's wings: Exodus 19.3–4
Moses then went up to God, and Yahweh called to him
from the mountain, saying, 'Say this to the House of
Jacob, declare this to the sons of Israel, "You yourselves
have seen what I did with the Egyptians, how I carried

you on eagle's wings and brought you to myself".'

A place of safety: Revelation 12.5–6, 13–17
The woman brought a male child into the world, the son
who was to rule all the nations with an iron sceptre, and
the child was taken straight up to God and to his throne,
while the woman escaped into the desert, where God had
made a place of safety ready, for her to be looked after in
the twelve hundred and sixty days.

   . . .

   As soon as the devil found himself thrown down to the
earth, he sprang in pursuit of the woman, the mother of
the male child, but she was given a huge pair of eagle's
wings to fly away from the serpent into the desert, to the
place where she was to be looked after for a year and twice
a year and half a year. So the serpent vomited water from
his mouth, like a river, after the woman, to sweep her
away in the current, but the earth came to her rescue; it
opened its mouth and swallowed the river thrown up by
the dragon's jaws. Then the dragon was enraged with the
woman and went away to make war on the rest of her children, that is, all who obey God's commandments and bear
witness for Jesus.

MEDITATION

The third Glorious Mystery of the Rosary turned our thoughts to the people of God, to the whole mystical body of Christ; the fourth and fifth Glorious Mysteries direct our minds to a single member of the mystical body, to Mary the mother of God. But Mary is not simply a single member of the Church. She is a singular member; from the moment of her conception she was distinguished from every other mortal by her being preserved from the stain of original sin; and this distinction continued throughout her whole life, for never once did she lose her unique status through the commission of any actual sin; finally her singularity was confirmed and rewarded by her exemption from bodily corruption. Soul and body, she passed from this world directly into the life of the Resurrection.

In reflecting on the mystery of the Annunciation and of the Visitation we have already considered the unique role our Lady played in the scheme of man's salvation. Her consent to the word proclaimed to her by the angel Gabriel was the response of a soul in the perfect condition in which almighty God had created mankind in the beginning, for what was required of her was an act that would correspond to, and counterbalance, the act of disobedience freely made by Eve. Eve's faithlessness, her acceptance of Satan's word in place of God's word prepared the way for the fall of mankind; Mary's faithfulness, her recognition that the angel's message was from God, and her believing the promise made to her, prepared the way for mankind's redemption, through the self-oblation of the second Adam, the Word made flesh in her womb.

There is a brief episode, recorded by Matthew, Mark, and Luke, which tells how our Lord reacted when told that his mother and kinsmen were waiting to see him. St Luke significantly links the episode with the parable of the Sower, which describes the different types of response men make to the word of God. Our Lord's immediate reaction was to say: 'My mother and my brothers are those who hear the word of God and put it into practice' (Luke 8.19–21), thus pointing to the essential quality that made Mary his mother: hearing and obeying the word of God. Similarly, discipleship consists in learning to practise the discernment and obedience which Mary had practised perfectly all her life.

Mary's act of obedience was a vital factor in the scheme of man's redemption, so vital that she can be said to have co-operated with God in the work of redemption. Near the end of the second century, Irenaeus, Bishop of Lyons, wrote: 'The knot of Eve's disobedience was untied by Mary's obedience. What the virgin Eve bound through her unbelief, Mary loosed by her faith'; and even more strongly: 'Being obedient, she became the cause of salvation for herself and for the whole human race.'

We must remember, of course, that Mary too was redeemed. As the Second Vatican Council (*Constitution on the Church*, n. 53) says: 'Because she belongs to the offspring of Adam she is one with all human beings in their need for salvation'. Her salvation, like that of all men, resulted from God's favour, and was accomplished through the merits of Christ's sacrifice, in her case applied from the moment of her conception; and the primary reason for her preservation from the decaying effects of sin was so that Christ could assume a perfect human nature. In Mary, who was fully redeemed by his own merits, he prepared a body for himself.

Her perfection of soul and body, however, conferred a unique privilege upon Mary herself. 'Because of this gift of sublime grace she far surpasses all other creatures, both in heaven and on earth' (*Constitution on the Church*, n. 53); and her passing directly from life upon earth to heavenly glory was the logical consequence of her sinlessness, of her fullness of grace. Having no stain of sin upon her, Mary had no need to pay the penalty of sin, which is death. She was able to pass immediately from the finitude of this life to the glorious life of the Resurrection. This is what is meant by Mary's assumption into heaven.

In earlier meditations we traced the Church's doctrine concerning our Lady back to Scripture, in particular to the gospel of the infancy presented by St Luke. We can now complete the picture by turning to one who, after our Lord, was closest to Mary, to the beloved disciple, St John, to whose care Mary was commended by her dying Son. St John went to live at Ephesus, and there, among the local congregation with whom our Lady lived, John or one of his close friends wrote the book of Revelation which, among its many visions, contains one which may well be John's pictorial expansion, on a cosmic canvas, of that never-to-be-forgotten scene at the foot of the cross, a scene with four characters: the Lord Jesus, Mary his mother, John representing all her other children, and lurking in the shadows the great enemy of mankind, the primeval serpent, the devil.

The vision referred to is contained in Revelation chapter 12, verses 1–6 and 13–17 (the intervening verses seem to be a separate vision). The title of the vision is announced in the last verse of chapter 11. 'The sanctuary of God in heaven opened, and the ark of the covenant could be seen inside it.' The ark of the new covenant is she who bears the Word of God.

The vision then opens with the appearance of a great sign in heaven: 'a woman, adorned with the sun, standing on the moon, and with the twelve stars on her head for a crown. She was pregnant, and in labour, crying aloud in the pangs of childbirth.' Here we have an allusion to Eve, who was to bring forth in pain and from whom one would come who would bruise the serpent's head. A dragon now appears and lies in wait to devour the child at birth; but the child is taken up to God and to his throne. The woman too escapes into the desert where God has prepared a place for her.

So far the vision is reminiscent of the Old Testament. Israel had given birth to the great leader Moses who escaped from the dragon of the Nile, Pharaoh, to be taken safely into the palace of the king, while eventually Israel herself escaped into the wilderness. The imagery can be applied not only to Moses but also to Christ and his Ascension to the Father. The image of the dragon lying in wait can thus be applied to Satan, seeking to destroy Christ, both at the moment of his birth (the slaughter of the innocents) and at the moment of his crucifixion.

With the escape of the child into heaven (Resurrection and Ascension) the attention of the dragon is turned back to the earth where he directs his attack upon the woman, who can now be seen to represent not just Eve or Israel but Mary. Now she too is safe, having been given eagle's wings to transport her to the desert. Eagle's wings represent the protection of God himself (Exodus 19.4; Deuteronomy 32.11). The woman has been removed from every possible assault of Satan by the intervention of God himself; she has been taken directly from earth to heaven. Although the woman is completely out of reach, the dragon, in a fury of frustration, vomits a river of water after her, but the river is swallowed up by the earth. This additional piece of action serves to underline the invulnerability the woman enjoys for as long as the world with its times of persecution lasts. In the first phase of the vision we were told that the woman would be safe for twelve hundred and sixty days. The persecution of the Jews by Antiochus Epiphanes had lasted that number of days, and so the number became the symbol for times of persecution, times which according to the book of Revelation will last as long as the world itself.

Enraged at his double failure, to destroy the child and to destroy his mother, Satan now begins to make war on 'the rest of her children'. The writer spells out for us who these are: 'All who obey God's commandments and bear witness for Jesus', that is, the whole Church on earth. These other children were represented at the foot of the cross by St John, the beloved disciple.

The vision, especially in its second phase, gives a unique distinction to 'the woman' in contrast to 'the rest of her children'. The 'rest of her children' live out their lives in the times of persecution that will recur throughout the world's history, whereas she, invulnerable to Satan's attack, already enjoys complete safety in a place prepared for her by God. Her assumption into heaven reflects the glory of the ascension of her child, who 'was taken straight up to God and to his throne', and is also a foreshadowing of the glory that will be granted at the proper time to 'the rest of her children', that is, to all who 'obey God's commandments and bear witness for Jesus.'

'THIS IS YOUR MOTHER': JOHN 19.25-7

Near the cross of Jesus stood his mother and his mother's sister, Mary the wife of Clopas, and Mary of Magdala. Seeing his mother and the disciple he loved standing near her, Jesus said to his mother, 'Woman, this is your son'. Then to the disciple he said, 'This is your mother'. And from that moment the disciple made a place for her in his home.

5

Crowning of Our Lady in Heaven

The highest honour of our race: Judith 13.18–20
Uzziah then said to Judith:

'May you be blessed, my daughter, by God Most High,
beyond all women on earth;
and may the Lord God be blessed,
the Creator of heaven and earth,
by whose guidance you cut off the head
of the leader of our enemies.
The trust you have shown
shall not pass from the memories of men,
but shall ever remind them
of the power of God.
God grant you to be always held in honour,
and rewarded with blessings,
since you did not consider your own life
when our nation was brought to its knees,
but warded off our ruin,
walking undeterred before our God.'

Queen of heaven and earth: Psalm 45.14–17
Dressed in brocades, the king's daughter
is led in to the king, with bridesmaids in her train.

Her ladies-in-waiting follow
and enter the king's palace to general rejoicing.

Your ancestors will be replaced by sons
whom you will make lords of the whole world.

I shall immortalise your name,
nations will sing your praises for ever and ever.

Sharing the divine nature: 2 Peter 1.3–11
By his divine power, he has given us all the things that we
need for life and for true devotion, bringing us to know
God himself, who has called us by his own glory and
goodness. In making these gifts, he has given us the guarantee of something very great and wonderful to come:
through them you will be able to share the divine nature
and to escape corruption in a world that is sunk in
vice. But to attain this, you will have to do your utmost
yourselves, adding goodness to the faith that you have,
understanding to your goodness, self-control to your
understanding, patience to your self-control, true devotion to your patience, kindness towards your fellow men
to your devotion, and, to this kindness, love. If you have
a generous supply of these, they will not leave you inef-
fectual or unproductive: they will bring you to a real
knowledge of our Lord Jesus Christ. But without them a
man is blind or else short-sighted; he has forgotten how
his past sins were washed away. Brothers, you have been
called and chosen: work all the harder to justify it. If you
do all these things there is no danger that you will ever
fall away. In this way you will be granted admittance into
the eternal kingdom of our Lord and saviour Jesus
Christ.

Each in his proper order: 1 Corinthians 15.20–3
But Christ has in fact been raised from the dead, the first-
fruits of all who have fallen asleep. Death came through
one man and in the same way the resurrection of the dead
has come through one man. Just as all men die in Adam,

so all men will be brought to life in Christ; but all of them in their proper order: Christ as the first-fruits and then, after the coming of Christ, those who belong to him.

Palms in their hands: Revelation 7.9–12
After that I saw a huge number, impossible to count, of people from every nation, race, tribe and language; they were standing in front of the throne and in front of the Lamb, dressed in white robes and holding palms in their hands. They shouted aloud, 'Victory to our God, who sits on the throne, and to the Lamb!' And all the angels who were standing in a circle round the throne, surrounding the elders and the four animals, prostrated themselves before the throne, and touched the ground with their foreheads, worshipping God with these words, 'Amen. Praise and glory and wisdom and thanksgiving and honour and power and strength to our God for ever and ever. Amen.'

MEDITATION

The heart of the Rosary is the great mystery of our Lord's redemptive action, manifested in the events that took place between the first Holy Thursday and Pentecost. That is why, after the first three Joyful Mysteries, our Lady falls more or less into the background, for her primary purpose, that of bearing the Redeemer of the world, has been fulfilled. It is fitting, however, that she returns in the last two Mysteries of the Rosary. She is the human framework around her Son's redemptive work. In the Annunciation we took note of how, by her perfect discernment of, and obedience to, the word of God she provided the human link in the chain of redemptive events; now we take note of her final reward: her Assumption into heaven, and her crowning as Queen of angels and saints.

In considering the final glory of our Lady, we ought first to observe that the honour did not issue from her own power but was conferred upon her. Christ, by the power of his own divinity, and by right, *ascended* to resume the glory that was his with the Father before time began; our Lady was *assumed* into heaven and given glory by divine favour, for 'she is one with all human beings in their need for salvation'. Second, we ought to observe that, although our Lady is one of the redeemed, there never was a moment in her life when she lost her immaculate state. This enabled her to anticipate the general resurrection, and enjoy perfect bliss of body and soul from the moment her life on earth was over. But in so doing she realized perfectly the goal towards which the whole

Church is moving. 'Therefore she is hailed as a pre-eminent and altogether singular member of the Church, and as the Church's model and excellent exemplar in faith and charity' (*Constitution on the Church*, n. 53).

The New Testament speaks in many places and in many phrases of the 'glory, as yet unrevealed, which is waiting for us' (Romans 8.18). It is no less than the radiance of the image of the Son of God. Of the redeemed St Paul writes: 'They are the ones he chose specially long ago and intended to become true images of his Son, so that his Son might be the eldest of many brothers. He called those he intended for this; those he called he justified, and with those he justified he shared his glory' (Romans 8.29–30). The New Testament speaks also of the transfiguration of our mortal bodies, so that the bodily Assumption of our Lady can be seen as an earnest of the resurrection of the other members of the mystical body of Christ. 'The dead will be raised, imperishable, and we shall be changed as well, because our present perishable nature must put on imperishability and this mortal nature must put on immortality' (1 Corinthians 15.52–3).

While venerating our Lady's pre-eminence among the redeemed we need not and must not see her in isolation. She is the supreme glory of the heavenly Jerusalem, but that city is a place where 'millions of angels have gathered for the festival, with the whole Church in which everyone is a "first-born son" and a citizen of heaven' (Hebrews 12.22).

The *Constitution on the Church* (n. 65) points out that 'In the most holy Virgin the Church has already reached that perfection whereby she exists without spot or wrinkle. Yet the followers of Christ still strive to increase in holiness by conquering sin.' In St John's vision of the woman adorned with the sun (Revelation 12.1–6, 13–17) we learned how the woman escaped to a place of complete safety, whereas the rest of her children, those other than Christ himself, were left to face the assaults of Satan. These persecutions will harass the Church until the end of time. 'Because you do not belong to the world, because my choice withdrew you from the world, therefore the world hates you' (John 15.19).

We tend to think of persecution as physical torments such as the early Christians suffered at the hands of the Roman empire. This is certainly part of what is meant, for such torment is a severe trial of faith, but it is more than that. St John, like the other New Testament writers, makes quite clear in his letters that the struggle with Satan goes on all the time in the soul, even when there is no apparent outward persecution; and the particular historical persecutions to which St John may allude in his Revelation thus become symbols of the constant interior persecution of the Church by Satan.

My children, do not let anyone lead you astray:
to live a holy life
is to be holy just as he is holy;
to lead a sinful life is to belong to the devil. (1 John 3.7–8)

Faith and baptism recreate our souls, but the struggle between the word of God and the empty promises of Satan goes on in our members until the final victory is won; and there can be no relaxation of vigilance for the individual until his own personal judgement is past, nor for the Church until the last day.

One of the most sustained exhortations to perseverance in faith and faithfulness is contained in the Letter to the Hebrews, beginning at chapter 11 with the familiar sentence: 'Only faith can guarantee the blessings that we hope for, or prove the existence of the realities that at present remain unseen.' The writer takes our thoughts right back to Abraham, father of the faithful, and sees, in the nomadic life he accepted in response to God's call, a symbol of the life of the Church. 'For there is no eternal city for us in this life but we look for one in the life to come' (Hebrews 13.14). Vitally important is this writer's stress on the source of true religion: recognizing and obeying the word of God. 'Make sure', he says, 'that you never refuse to listen when he speaks' Hebrews 12.25). This was precisely how Abraham proved himself, and was rewarded by becoming the father of a vast nation, the most illustrious member of which was Mary who in her time displayed the qualities of her ancestor in a pre-eminent degree. She discerned and obeyed the word of God, spoken to her by the angel, and she became the mother of an even vaster nation, of the whole Church of God. Blessed as she had been in her ancestor, she has become even more blessed in her offspring, first of whom was no other than the Son of the Most High God.

Your ancestors will be replaced by sons
whom you will make lords of the whole world.

(Psalm 45.16)

Let us conclude our meditation on the Mysteries with the thought of the universal motherhood of Mary. Her accepting motherhood of the Redeemer was a necessary link in the scheme of our salvation, 'the cause of salvation' as St Irenaeus so strongly expressed it. So too she continues to perform a maternal office in the life of 'the rest of her children'. Her perpetual intercession is a vital link in the process of their sanctification. The Second Vatican Council teaches that Mary's maternity 'will last without interruption until the eternal fulfilment of all the elect. For, taken up to heaven, she did not lay aside this saving role, but by her manifold acts of intercession continues to win for us gifts of eternal salvation' (*Constitution on the Church*, n. 62). The same Council document reminds us that 'The maternal duty of Mary in no way obscures or diminishes this unique mediation of Christ, but rather shows its power. For all the saving influences of the Blessed Virgin on men originate, not from some inner necessity, but from the divine pleasure. They flow forth from the superabundance of the merits of Christ.' (n. 60).

We ought never to forget that, as St John tells us, the first 'sign' our Lord performed, by which he 'let his glory be seen', the changing of water into wine at the wedding-feast at Cana, was performed at his mother's request. This 'sign' is of the deepest significance. It was a declaration of the essence of redemption, a prelude to our Lord's whole ministry. 'They have no wine': the human race, even the chosen people, had lost the joy of the life of grace. Our Lord pointed out that his 'hour' had not come; only when that 'hour' had struck could mankind's privation be made good. That 'hour' was the hour of his glorification on the cross. None the less at the wedding feast he gave a 'sign' that this restoration would be accomplished. At this first glimpse of his glory his divine action followed his mother's intercession. That in itself was a sign of his mother's part in the scheme of redemption.

If our Lord did not feel his power and glory diminished by responding to her compassionate request, why should we hesitate to invoke that same interceding love in order to obtain, not just this or that trivial favour, but the wine of supernatural life in full measure, the perfect sanctification of our souls, and the redemption of the whole world?

There is another consideration which should move us to be quick to seek the intercession of Mary the mother of God. The first face that the Lord Jesus recognized was the face of his mother, Mary, and like every infant it was to his mother that he cried for help in all his needs. If he, her firstborn, cried to her for help, why should not we, her adopted children seek her help in our times of need? In doing so we are imitating Christ.

Holy Mary, mother of God, pray for us sinners, now and at the hour of our death.

A WOMAN, ADORNED WITH THE SUN:
REVELATION 11.19 – 12.1A

Then the sanctuary of God in heaven opened,
and the ark of the covenant could be seen
inside it. Then came flashes of lightning, peals
of thunder and an earthquake, and violent
hail.
Now a great sign appeared in heaven: a
woman, adorned with the sun, standing on the
moon, and with the twelve stars on her head
for a crown.